S0-ARN-901

Stevensville MD 21666-4026

MEMOIRS OF A MAIN STREET BOY

GROWING UP IN AMERICA'S ANCIENT CITY

RALPH W. CROSBY

ANAPHORA LITERARY PRESS

AUGUSTA, GEORGIA

Kent Island Branch
Queen Anne's County Library
200 Library circle
Stevensville MD 21666-4026

11/17

ANAPHORA LITERARY PRESS
2419 Southdale Drive
Hephzibah, GA 30815
http://anaphoraliterary.com

Book design by Anna Faktorovich, Ph.D.

Copyright © 2016 by Ralph W. Crosby

All rights reserved. No part of this book may be reproduced in any form or by
any electronic or mechanical means, including information storage and retrieval
systems, without permission in writing from Ralph W. Crosby. Writers are welcome
to quote brief passages in their critical studies, as American copyright law dictates.

Printed in the United States of America, United Kingdom and in Australia on acid-
free paper.

Cover Design by Belinda C. Butler.

Published in 2016 by Anaphora Literary Press

Memoirs of a Main Street Boy: Growing Up in America's Ancient City
Ralph W. Crosby—1st edition.

Library of Congress Control Number: 2016941194

Library Cataloging Information
Crosby, Ralph W., 1933-, author.
    Memoirs of a Main Street boy : Growing up in America's ancient city /
    Ralph W. Crosby
    230 p. ; 9 in.
    Includes bibliographical references and index.
    ISBN 978-1-68114-271-5 (hardcover : alk. paper)
    ISBN 978-1-68114-272-2 (softcover : alk. paper)
    ISBN 978-1-68114-273-9 (e-book)
1. Biography & Autobiography—Personal Memoirs. 2. Biography &
Autobiography—Business. 3. Biography & Autobiography—Historical—General.
E176-176.8: United States: History: Biography.
920: Biography, genealogy & insignia.

MEMOIRS OF A MAIN STREET BOY

GROWING UP IN AMERICA'S ANCIENT CITY

_____

RALPH W. CROSBY

The annals of the brave, intelligent, chivalrous people who made the City of Annapolis celebrated, are part of the history of the nation.

The Ancient City
Elihu S. Riley, 1887

The town is, in our tale, called "Gopher Prairie, Minnesota." But its Main Street is the continuation of Main Streets everywhere. The story would be the same in Ohio or Montana, in Kansas or Kentucky or Illinois, and not very differently would it be told up York State or in the Carolina hills. Main Street is the climax of civilization.

Main Street
Sinclair Lewis, 1920

CONTENTS

In memory of Lillian and Raymond Crosby, my mom and dad, who made our third-floor apartment more than a place to live—a home to remember.

PREFACE

In 1887, the printer-historian Elihu Riley wrote the then definitive history of Annapolis, Maryland. He called the town and his book *The Ancient City*. Riley's book chronicled Annapolis' pivotal role as one of America's early settlements and its role in the Revolution. In his introduction, Riley wrote of the "Revolutionary epoch:"

"In it, no city in the colonies was more prompt and decisive in resisting the aggressions of the crown, and in supplying troops and sinews of war for carrying on active operations in the field against British forces."

Since 1887, Annapolis has evolved and endured as a city of "national character," as Riley called it.

As a once thriving port city, it received the seafood bounty of the Chesapeake Bay—oysters, fish and crabs—to feed millions, and it also received, sadly, bullied and beaten Africans into slavery.

As Riley observed, in its second century, Annapolis was revitalized as home of the United States Naval Academy, producing new patriots who would fight to keep the country free. Its other college, St. Johns, would produce the writer of our national anthem and become the acclaimed purveyor of education based on the world's great books.

Through it all, the illustrious homes of the revolutionary patriots, the inns and meeting halls where the nation's founders met and lived, were preserved and restored. You can still walk the halls where Washington, Jefferson, Franklin, and their comrades planned war and made peace.

This geography and these institutions were the learning places and playgrounds of my youth. If, indeed, "the child is father of the man," then Annapolis had a great influence on that paternity.

Throughout an early career as a journalist in Baltimore, Maryland, and Washington, D.C., and a later longer career as founder and owner of a national advertising/public relations agency, Annapolis has remained home.

But this book is not an autobiography. It is a memoir about growing up in one of the most disruptive yet most dynamic eras of our nation's history—from the end of the Great Depression, through World War II, to the Cold War—and how that impacted my generation on Main Streets across America.

Sinclair Lewis, in his esteemed novel *Main Street*, called his fictional town Gopher Prairie's Main Street, "the continuation of Main Streets everywhere." The only difference in my Main Street is the significance of its place in American history and the people, places and events that made it significant. This book is as much about them as it is about me and my generation.

—Ralph W. Crosby
Annapolis, Maryland

CHAPTER ONE

VIEWING THE WORLD FROM
A THIRD FLOOR APARTMENT

I'm what is called an "Annapolitan"—born, raised and always with a home in Annapolis, Maryland.

"Annapolitan" seems redolent of "Cosmopolitan" and sounds a bit pretentious for those who live in such a small town. Cosmopolitan or "cultured" might have fit Annapolis in the 18th Century, but certainly not in the 20th. It's also hard to give undue importance to a boy growing up on Main Street, the two-and-a-half block commercial center of Annapolis, especially a youngster living in a third floor, walk-up apartment during what were, to paraphrase Charles Dickens, "the best of times, the worst of times."

The worst of times because I was born in the latter part of the "Great Depression," December 16, 1933, to be exact, and spent a youth punctuated by wars—the Second World War, the Cold War and the Korean War.

The best of times—being a youngster in a town surrounded by fish-and-crab-filled creeks and rivers snaking off the Chesapeake Bay, where you could walk to those waters to swim and fish, walk to school, walk to the library or to the ball fields and gymnasiums of St. John's College and the United States Naval Academy. I walked to them all.

When I was four years old, my mom, dad and I moved to the third floor apartment at 183 Main Street, where I would live for the next 20 years.

As a young child, that apartment seemed like a huge place. Only when I reached my teen years, having experienced the larger homes of some friends, did I realize how small it was. But through all the years, it had the sweet experience, then memories, of "home" and all that word means to those who love family and neighborhood.

"Neighborhood" had a lot to do with the experience, because mine was rich in small town closeness and the magic of colonial American history rivaled only by Boston and Philadelphia.

The apartment at 183 Main Street was like so many others of the day, situated above the stores on the main business street.

"Main Street," of course, has taken on special significance in the U.S., a generic representation of all small town central retail streets, even representing small business people as opposed to "Wall Street" as representative of big business. Like those in other small towns, my Main Street reflected the street life of the city, with holiday parades; Saturday night walkers, drinkers and shoppers; auto-owner showoffs; movie goers; and Sunday church goers. Being raised at 183 Main Street put me at the epicenter of small town life.

You entered 183 from a door-wide set of three steps located between a dress shop and a stationery store. Climbing two long dark flights of stairs, you entered the apartment into a long hall with several rooms off it, including the "front room," or living room. The front room, of course, faced Main Street, and through its large windows I could watch my small world go by and imagine some of the greatest events of the American Revolution that unfolded nearby.

Living on Main Street made you somewhat immune to sounds—such as car horns blasting each other, except for the older cars, whose distinguishing horns emitted an "ooga, ooga" rather than the more shrill bugle call. In summer, with screens in the windows, even conversations wafted up to the third floor, and there were always kids yelling as they played. The sound that penetrated was the siren of a fire truck from the station on nearby Duke of Gloucester Street as it sped through the downtown. It's remarkable how these trucks could maneuver through narrow streets built for horse and buggy travel.

The front room had a sofa, two stuffed chairs and an upright radio console, with a rug on the floor where I would lay listening to Sammy Baugh lead the Washington Redskins into a pro football battle or the Lone Ranger, riding "the great horse Silver," with his Indian companion Tonto at his side, routing another bunch of bad guys. The radio had buttons you pushed to select a station. It even had one labeled "television," though we had no idea what that was.

The apartment consisted of five other rooms, two bedrooms, a dining room, a tiny bathroom and a not-much-bigger kitchen. There was a pantry off the kitchen housing a refrigerator and shelves for canned goods and other foodstuffs. With a stove, a sink, a table that could fit the three of us—for I was an only child—and a hot water heater and radiator, you could only move through the kitchen one person at a time.

The hot water heater or boiler had to be lit every time you wanted to take a bath. You also had to be sure to turn off the gas so the boiler wouldn't get too hot and explode. In the bathroom, there was only a tub—no shower. I didn't know what a shower was until around age nine when I started playing basketball in the high school gym.

The bathroom was so tiny that by the time my mother got her first washing machine, you had to pull in your stomach to get to the sink or toilet. Of course, in my younger days I remember my mother hunched over the bathtub washing clothes on a scrub board. When she did get a washing machine, it had to be hooked up to the spigots on the sink and had a wringer that you hand fed your washed clothing to press out the water—at the risk of crushed fingers.

Off the kitchen were the back stairs and the entrance to my favorite place as a child—the back porch. Only about 12 feet by 20 feet, it was a place of learning and a place of fantasy. It even supplied Seckel pears from the tree in the yard next door, which I could reach with my long-handled crab net. The fact that the yard next door was the side yard of an historic 18th century home was lost on me until many years later.

So, that apartment was my everyday home until I went off to college at 18 and my back-from-school home until I was 24 and got married.

One-third of the way from the top of the street, the apartment's two large front windows presented a special view of my world. If you leaned out one of the windows, with your knees on the floor, you could survey all of Main Street and even see above the buildings across the street and glimpse some of Annapolis' historic highlights.

Just a seven to eight minute stroll from top to bottom, Main Street is bounded at the top by the round-about road called Church Circle, dominated in its center by historic St. Anne's Episcopal Church, and at its bottom by the venerable city dock, structured remains of the harbor that originally defined the city.

In the early 1700s, Main Street was a block shorter than in my day because the "dock," originally a synonym for harbor, extended haphazardly higher into the city. But the link of this maritime economic engine of the area with the power base of the colonies, represented by the Protestant St. Anne's Church, gave Main Street significance beyond Annapolis.

The Main Street of my youth, c. 1935, looking from the city dock area to St. Anne's Church. To the right, the dome of Maryland's State House juts above the stores. (Collection of the Maryland State Archives)

Our apartment was on the left side of the street going up, so that if I looked out the front window two blocks to the right would be the city dock with its waterman's workboats, an occasional pleasure craft and, in the background, where the Chesapeake Bay fed into the Severn River, dots of white and grey as sailboats frolicked and workboats plied their trade, fishing, crabbing and oystering the bountiful waters. Sometimes, the dock was so filled with skipjacks and other workboats, you could walk across its narrow head—some 50 to 60 feet wide—using boats secured side-by-side as stepping stones.

The landing side of the dock, shrunk considerably from its colonial port size, in my youth and now, mimics the size of a football field, spreading out somewhat in length and width as it exits into the river. (See map on the following page.)

Sailing out of the dock and tacking starboard, you enter Spa Creek which, in my youth, was the eastern boundary of the city. On the Creek, you sail past the manor house of Charles Carrol of Carrollton, one of the most venerated signers of the U.S. Declaration of Independence, and into the waters of my boyhood adventures and misadventures.

If you sail out of the dock to the port side, you'll be at the seawall of the U.S. Naval Academy, which hugs the broad, Severn River, bounded landside by parade grounds and sports fields, for midshipmen marching and ball-playing and playgrounds for me and my young pals.

ANNAPOLIS - *At the time of these memoirs*

1 183 Main Street *2* State House *3* St. Anne's Church *4* City Dock

5 ⬤St. Mary's Church and ◼Charles Carroll of Carrollton House *6* ⬤Naval Academy Chapel

A Chesapeake Bay workboat delivering oysters at the Annapolis city dock.
(Collection of the Maryland State Archives)

From my window, on a clear day, as you look past the harbor, you could see across the Bay to the outline of the Eastern Shore of Maryland, some four or five miles away. Leaning out the window, if you panned from the Bay over the city you'd see several of the hallmark spires that rose over Annapolis, beacons of American history.

Chapter Two

Beacons of History

L ooking dockward out my front window, the first spires to arise are the radio towers on Greenbury Point, the peninsula on the north side of the Severn River, where it meets the Bay, across from the Naval Academy.

Greenbury Point, often referred to aptly as "North Severn," was home to the Navy's Engineering Experiment Station that tested Naval equipment, from the first biplane to modern jet engines. The towers, which dominated the skyline entering the Bay, were erected in 1918 to support a high powered radio station as a First World War precaution to keep communications open with Europe if the enemy cut undersea cables. The communications capacity at North Severn was greatly expanded in World War II to become the primary transmitting station to Navy ships deployed around the world.

The towers were landmarks for Bay watermen since they could be seen from miles away, and for my father, who saw them being erected, they meant home whenever he returned from trips out of town, which were few and far between. Many times, I heard him say, "I never want to get so far away from Annapolis that I can't see the radio towers."

Greenbury Point was also the place where the Puritans, Virginia immigrants who would create Annapolis, first settled in the 1649-1650 timeframe before moving to the south side of the Severn River. (The more purist local historians don't like using "Puritans" to describe these immigrants who settled along the Severn. The Puritans were only one brand of English dissenters, discontented with the Church of England, who escaped persecution from church leaders and the King by immigrating to America. With that understood, I'll use "Puritan" as the simplest descriptor for these Severn area settlers.)

Panning farther left, you'd see the top of the copper dome of the Naval Academy Chapel, weathered to a green patina, and directly over the buildings across from 183 Main Street would rise the majestic wooden dome of the Maryland State House, one of the nation's most historic buildings. (I'll have more to say later about these two basilicas.) Then, looking to the left up Main Street, the gothic steeple of St. Anne's acted as an arrow pointing skyward from the center of the City.

At the center of the city, St. Anne's Episcopal Church sits where it was designed to be located when Annapolis was laid out in 1696.

In size and appearance, the church is not cathedral-like. In fact, it is small by most standards. But it is a stately, brick structure that rises about three stories high, at least a floor higher than its neighbors in my youth. Its steeple can be seen from blocks away and the tower holds four town clocks one each facing the four main points of the compass.

While knowing the time of day, especially since the church bells rang on the quarter hour, was convenient for most, these clocks took away my boyhood lateness excuse, "I didn't know what time it was." Though I didn't own a watch, my mother knew I was playing seldom more than a few blocks from Church Circle and easily could have checked the clocks.

From Church Circle, lining both sides of Main Street to the dock, the shops and civic establishments supplied almost everything a family needed to live.

Where Church Circle first meets Main Street, on the 183 side, stands the Maryland Inn, built in 1782, lodging and feeding guests, especially legislators, then and now. In my day, across the street opposite the Inn was Annapolis Banking and Trust Company, a local institution where my mother spent a short while as a teller in one of her many jobs and where, as an adult, I would serve on its Board of Directors for a long while, 26 years, before it was sold to a larger bank.

If you scanned Main Street from top to bottom, the store signs hung out over the sidewalks like colorful flags of different shapes vying for attention among the electric poles and utility lines that crisscrossed the street. To be honest, the poles and lines spoiled the view to the dock or St. Anne's; they were distractions, like food stains on a clean, white shirt. In those days, I would have agreed with one of Sinclair Lewis' characters in his novel *Main Street*: "I do admit that Main Street is not as beautiful as it should be." (Thankfully, by the mid-1990s the signs over sidewalks were legislated away and the utility lines went underground, making Main Street much more beautiful than in my youth.)

The store signs shouted "Shoe Store;" "Men's-Ladies Wear;" "Public Loan Office" emblazoned with its pawn shop balls; "Furniture," "Rexall Drugs;" and restaurant names galore.

Main Street restaurants became personal havens over the years. I played chess with the proprietor in a tiny eatery called The New Grill; put too many nickels in the pinball machines in the Wardroom Restaurant; kept a few nickels for late evening ten-cents-a-piece hamburgers at the Little Tavern; took my earliest dates for pizza at LaRosa's; and met my high school chums after school at the dining area at the rear of Read's Drug Store.

Main Street boasted not one but two five and ten cent stores, Murphy's at the foot of Main Street and Woolworth's, a bit up and across from 183. What I remember most about both were the open displays of candy inside their doors, and I must admit to some sticky fingers as I passed these enticing rows of sweets, especially coveting one of my favorites, a Mary Jane or a Bit-O-Honey.

Just up the street from Woolworth's was the Maggio family's fruit and vegetable store, with the grandiose name "Annapolis Fruit and Produce Company," where I cleaned up and stocked food for one summer as a youngster. The tiny store, run by two older immigrants from Italy and overseen by their entrepreneurial son, Tony, was distinguished by the peanut roasting machine that stood out front on the sidewalk. A bulky, metal machine that used a strip heater to roast the peanuts, it produced warm nuts in their shells that had a distinct taste I haven't experienced since.

Beyond Maggio's was a doorway with white columns with the letters above it proclaiming B.P.O.E. We would joke that stood for "Best People on Earth," rather than "Benevolent Protective Order of Elks." The joke satisfied me since my dad was a member and, through the years, it became an entertainment center for me, as well—from a place to watch football on television, since we didn't own a set until my late teens, to the sponsor of my one summer camp in the mountains of Western Maryland, to dances with my mother when I'd stop in the Elks on Saturday night in my late teens.

My area of Main Street when we moved there in the mid-1930s, including my favorite entertainment spot, the Republic Theater. My family's third floor apartment window is visible at the far left. A few years later, the building on the other side of the Republic would be razed for the parking lot I used as a playground. (Collection of the Maryland State Archives)

My biggest formal entertainment spot was one building up from our apartment—the Republic Movie Theater, another place where both my mother and I worked for short stints—she as a ticket seller and I as an usher. And the movie house had a parking lot next door, where we played ball and ate grapes off the fence in the rear of the lot. Grapes in a parking lot, pears, apples or cherries for picking on nearby neighborhood trees—all seemed quite natural in those days in Annapolis. The "movie lot," as we called it, sat next to the massive concrete wall of the theater. I used that wall as a backboard to play catch with myself with a lacrosse ball and stick, lacrosse being a traditional Maryland sport that I would play in high school and college.

There were at least three grocery stores on Main Street, plus a meat market, a bakery, jewelers, stationers, gift shops, hat stores, several pharmacies, and the offices and sales floor of the Gas and Electric Company.

We even had an Amoco gas station at the foot of Main Street in the middle of the traffic circle adjacent to the city dock.

Some buildings had signs painted on their sides, such as "Genuine Bull Durham Tobacco" for roll-your-own cigarettes or "Credit" on the furniture store wall. Many had awnings out front that could be cranked open to shield patrons from the rain or sun. Those awnings, red, green, blue or striped, made Main Street more colorful, if not beautiful.

Most of these first-floor stores were topped with one or two floors of living space, like 183, the general plan for apartment living for working-class Annapolitans.

Those windows of 183 witnessed many an event both monumental and simply personal. For example, it was those windows, covered by dark shades to keep from revealing light that theoretically might attract bombers in World War II, which were thrown open to hear the sounds of paper boys shouting "Extra. Extra. The War is over" in 1945. On the more trivial and personal level, it was through those windows that my mother watched me cross the street to the grocery store and emerge with a candy bar that she knew I had no money to pay for. I was six or seven and received a lesson in honesty and apology as well as a sore behind.

Looking down to the right, I might see my friends gathered on the stone steps of the house next door. Those three broad, stone steps were our "street corner," where we'd guess the makes of cars going up Main Street or debate the baseball greatness of Ted Williams versus Joe DiMaggio.

Of course, like many things in Annapolis, those stone steps had historic significance. They led to the side entrance of what was known in colonial times as the Carroll Barrister House, built in the early 1720s and home of the patriot Charles Carroll the Barrister, who was born there in 1724.

Carroll the Barrister fought the infamous stamp and tea taxes, led a boycott of British goods, served in the Continental Congress and was the principal writer of the Declaration of Delegates of Maryland, at the same time with the same purpose as our Declaration of Independence.

The Carroll Barrister House and 183 Main Street next door, in the mid-1930s around the time we moved into our third floor apartment. (See arrow). (Courtesy of the Library of Congress)

The house, itself, one of the great surviving examples of 18th Century architecture, not only gave me and my pals a stoop for gathering, but its yard supplied me with those tasty Seckel pears from its ancient tree. My mother watched from our front windows in 1955 when the old house was torn from its foundation and carted up Main Street to its current home on the St. Johns College campus. It soon would be replaced by, of all things, a Burger King.

On any weekday shortly after 5 p.m., I could look out the window to see my dad walking home from his job as a sheet metal worker at the Naval Academy and see him stop at the pool room on Main Street for his perennial ten-cent glass of beer before heading home for dinner.

I could also watch midshipmen marching from the Naval Academy, whether it was on Sunday to church or celebrating a football win over Army. The street cleared as the blue-suited, white-capped brigade members moved in perfect unison to the "Hut, One, Two, Three, Hut" call. Among them could have been future President James Earl Carter (Class of 1946); Astronaut Alan Shepard (Class of 1944), the first American to travel in space; Walter (Wally) Schirra, Jr. (Class of 1945), along with Shepard, one of the original seven Mercury Astronauts, and the one I would interview as a young newspaper reporter right after he was chosen as an astronaut.

Marching by my window would be numerous future Naval heroes who would fight our wars, and also sports heroes, several of whom, later in life, became my friends—as would several who were later imprisoned during the Vietnam War. Annapolis, the city, had a way of getting into the hearts of many midshipmen, and they returned to our town to live, especially in retirement.

Back in Time

Now, suppose my living room window had been a time machine, able to take me back to Annapolis in the 1700s. I might have seen the Sons of Liberty, a group of distinguished patriots, leaving a Church Street hostelry for the State House, preparing to declare independence from Great Britain, fight a revolutionary war, and write a Declaration of Independence and a constitution. Or I might look up toward Church Circle in 1784 and see members of the Continental Congress walking from the State House to the Maryland Inn for a celebratory drink after ratifying the Treaty of Paris, the treaty that officially ended the war for independence. Around 1784, I also might have seen two future presidents, Thomas Jefferson and James Monroe, leaving their rented house near Church Circle to do business on Main Street (then called Church Street).

Earlier, in 1781, I could have seen the Marquis de Lafayette and his lieutenants entering a Church Street hostelry to dine after leaving their American troops bivouacked across Spa Creek from Annapolis.

Even earlier, in 1774, in a popular inn on upper Church Street called the "Coffee House," you might have encountered, on his way to Williamsburg, one Patrick Henry, a Virginia assemblyman held high in esteem by all those who sought independence from Great Britain.

It was Henry, who on March 23, 1775, would speak those words that would stir his compatriots then and stir most of us as far back as Grammar school:

"Is life so dear, or peace so sweet, as to be purchased at the price of chains and slavery? Forbid it, Almighty God! I know not what course others may take, but as for me, give me liberty, or give me death!"

With such a time machine, I could jump forward to 1789 and watch the 10-year-old Francis Scott Key cross Church Street on his way to King Williams School, which would become St. John's College, from which Key would graduate as one of its accomplished academics and amateur poets and a soon-to-be lawyer. This same young man would find himself in 1814 watching "bombs bursting in air that gave proof through the night that our flag was still there" on a ship off Baltimore's Fort McHenry.

More personally, I could see back to around 1730 and watch my great-great-great-great-great grandfather Burden Crosby, Commander of *The George*, bring his ship into the Annapolis harbor, picking up tobacco to transport to London.

Our mythical time machine could also show ancient sights you might not like to see. Besides ships that brought some of the nation's founders to Annapolis and ones that carried tobacco to England returning with all types of goods, you would see ships of agony docking in Annapolis harbor—slave ships that brought to America chained, sickened Africans such as famed author Alex Haley's ancestor, Kunta Kinte, immortalized in Haley's book *Roots*.

One of the most inspirational scenes we could view through our window time machine would be that of a large white horse carrying a tall man, with powdered hair and militarily dress with a cape over his shoulder to fend off the December 23, 1783 chill, leaving a Church Street hotel for the State House. The man was George Washington, on his way to take the momentous action of resigning his commission as Commander In Chief of the Continental Army, a decision described by one biographer, and echoed by many, as "the most significant address ever delivered to a civil society."

Chapter Three

George Washington (and I) Slept Here

From the time I was born until I was four, when we moved to 183 Main Street, we lived half a block away, around the corner and across the street at 167 Conduit Street. Located at the corner of Main and Conduit above a clothing store facing Main Street, this apartment was directly across the street from the Carroll Barrister house's front entrance. You could look out the window of our second floor apartment and view the stately Carroll home with its black, wrought iron fence encompassing a yard of ancient boxwoods. How often through the years I brushed those furry feeling, green-leafed boxwoods with my hand as I turned off Main to Conduit and on to nearby adventure and mischief.

As with so many downtown properties, much history surrounded the apartment on Conduit Street (so named because it was built to provide passage, or a conduit, from Church Street to Duke of Gloucester Street, the latter honoring Prince William, Duke of Gloucester, son of Queen Anne of Great Britain, from whom Annapolis got its name).

The lot where the apartment house stands clearly shows on the first map of the town to survive, a 1718 plat drawn by one James Stoddart, which lists the lot as number 46 owned by Amos Garrett. Garrett, an English-born merchant of considerable means, became the first mayor of the newly chartered town in 1708.

The property was later sold to Henrietta Dulany, matriarch of the eminent Dulany family, which held many of the provincial government's major positions. Her son, Lloyd Dulany, built a large, very expansive house on the property around 1770 and lived there until the fateful year, 1776, when his British loyalist leanings forced him to flee Maryland for England aboard the aptly named ship "Annapolis." Like the properties of many citizens who remained loyal to the British Crown and left the country, Dulany's property was confiscated by the state government in 1781 and auctioned off.

The property was purchased by innkeeper George Mann, who turned it into a successful tavern and hotel frequented by the rich and famous of the day. In the nineteenth century the tavern flourished under the name "City Hotel." When it closed in 1900, part of it was converted into the Colonial Theater for plays and viewing some of the early "moving pictures." The theater burned down in 1919, and the apartment house was built shortly thereafter, some ten years before we moved in.

The arrow points to Mann's Tavern, at Main and Conduit Streets, around 1891 after it became The City Hotel. The original was George Washington's favorite Annapolis hostelry. (Collection of the Maryland State Archives)

Since we lived there in my earliest years, I don't remember much about that apartment, though, later, I got a few tidbits from my mother. She told me that on one very hot summer night she and my dad went downstairs and out front to cool off, leaving me, a baby, asleep on their bed. Hearing my sudden, loud crying through the second floor window, they rushed upstairs to find me in a pool of blood. I had managed to roll off the bed and cut open my chin on the radiator, little the worse off, except for the slight scar I carry with me to this day. It was not my chin, but the bedroom on the second floor that makes this story noteworthy.

It was in a nearby bedroom spot, 150 years earlier on December 23, 1783, in Mann's Tavern that George Washington also spent a fitful night, his mind occupied with the next day's events—or his stomach bothered by the copious food and drink consumed at the evening's celebratory dinner and ball in his honor.

Washington arrived in Annapolis on December 19 for the purpose of resigning formally as Commander-In-Chief of the Continental Army, returning his commission to the Congress, then meeting in the State House. He was greeted by thirteen cannon blasts and escorted to George Mann's Tavern for his stay.

These were familiar surroundings for Washington; his footprints were all over Annapolis, in its homes, halls and taverns. Even Mann's Tavern was familiar since, in the early 1770s, he was a guest there when the house belonged to Lloyd Dulany and both men were loyal British subjects.

Records show that Washington was in Annapolis as early as 1757 and visited many times thereafter. We know from his diaries that in 1771 Washington dined at the Duke of Gloucester Street home of Charles Carroll of Carrollton, the richest man in the colonies and the only Catholic signer of the Declaration of Independence. Washington probably visited across Conduit Street from Mann's at the house of patriot Charles Carroll the Barrister, by then occupied by Carroll's sister, Mary Clare, and her family. (There were so many Charles Carrolls around that the distant cousins, Carrollton and the Barrister, had an appendage after their names to distinguish one Charles from the other.)

In Annapolis, Washington was much less the military man and much more the landed socialite and social gambler. He often attended the horse races held in Annapolis and enjoyed playing cards with the town's gentry. His diaries record bets he made and money he lost on those bets. He also enjoyed the well-known local theater, noting the four plays he saw and three balls he attended during the eight-day stay in Annapolis in 1771.

On his various visits to Annapolis, Washington frequented other taverns, some of which still exist, including Middleton Tavern,

Horatio Middleton's hostel for seafarers next to the city dock, and the Maryland Inn.

One historic meeting in the city that Washington decided not to attend was the 1786 Annapolis Convention, which was called to discuss commercial issues between the states that threatened the new nation. While the Annapolis Convention was a failure (only five states were represented), the delegates scheduled the 1787 Convention in Philadelphia that created the U.S. Constitution. The delegates met to make this momentous decision in—of all places—Washington's favorite hostelry, Mann's Tavern.

Washington did stop in Annapolis on his way to Philadelphia about a month after his war-ending victory over the British at Yorktown, and he was celebrated with two days of appreciation events. *The Maryland Gazette* reported, "People of every rank and every age eagerly pressed forward to feed their eyes with gazing on the man, to whom, under Providence... they owed their present security, and their hopes of future liberty and peace."

So, it was in familiar territory that Washington came to resign his commission as Commander-in-Chief of the Continental Army.

Congress decided that the hero of the Revolution should be honored with a grand dinner on December 22 and resign at noon the next day. The dinner, attended by several hundred of the country's and Annapolis' elite and catered by George Mann, was extravagant for any era. Mann not only supplied food and drink, including 98 bottles of wine and two-and-a-half gallons of "spirits," but also the musicians, waiters, twelve packs of cards to play with for those who didn't dance, and eight pounds of candles. The drinks were required for the 13 toasts to everything from "The Virtuous Daughters of America" (toast number 11) to "Long Health and Happiness to our illustrious General" (toast number 13). Each toast was followed by the loud roar of 13 cannons stationed on State House hill. A grand ball in the State House followed dinner, and Washington is said to have danced every minuet and reel.

During his stay, Washington visited many Annapolis friends. He even got a shave in a barber shop on nearby Cornhill Street.

Arising in his second floor bedroom at Mann's Tavern the morning of December 23, Washington dressed in his military uniform one more time. At six foot three inches in height, with large hands and feet, and weighing about 185 pounds, he was considered a giant of a man in an age when the average height of an English male was about five foot five inches. With ramrod straight posture, he was an imposing figure dressed in his buff and deep blue uniform with its shiny, brass buttons and his sword at his side.

That morning, after reviewing a draft of the retirement arrangements, prepared under the guidance of Thomas Jefferson, and a look at his speech, Washington decided to take time to write a letter to a dear friend, Baron von Steuben, who had served as the General's Chief of Staff in the final years of the Revolutionary War. A major general in the Continental Army, von Steuben taught the mostly untrained American soldiers military drills and tactics that would serve them well in battle. Washington wrote:

"This is the last letter I shall ever write while I continue the service of my country; the hour of my resignation is fixed at twelve this day; after which I shall become a private citizen on the Banks of the Potomack..."

Just before noon, Washington put the retirement documents in his pocket and headed off to meet Congress, riding his horse across Church Street, seeing the City Dock on his right and St. Anne's Church on his left, taking the short trip up the hill to the State House.

State House Hill

In my childhood, I made that same trek from Main Street to State House hill countless times. That spot was selected in 1695 for government house because it was the highest in town and, on its east front, presented a view down to the harbor.

The hill, surrounded by a roundabout street called State Circle, was grassy and full of historic relics and statuary. It became a welcome playground for us youngsters. The hill was great for rolling down in summer and sledding down on snowy winter days. When we were a bit older, as cars crept around the snow covered circle, we'd belly flop on our sleds behind them, grab a bumper and get a free ride around the circle, sometimes with snow in the face if the car had chains to grip the slick surface, in those days before snow tires. Little did we realize then the danger in that ride even though a few bloody noses resulted.

I first went to play on State House hill when I was six or seven, having proven I could cross the street safely. The proof came from walking to school. My mother walked me to grammar school for much of the first grade, but after that considerable practice, she let me go on my own. Since Annapolis Grammar School was on Green Street, one long block down Main or Duke of Gloucester, it was undoubtedly a safe trip. There were lights for crossing at both Conduit and Main and Conduit and Duke of Gloucester, and when you reached Green Street a crossing guard was on duty. The light at Conduit also allowed me to cross Main Street, and alleys between the stores led to State Circle.

The Maryland State House with Roger Brooke Taney's statue in front.

When I got to State House hill, it was like going to a park, and the statues turned into jungle gyms. My favorite statue to climb was that of Roger Brooke Taney, (originally pronounced Taw-nee, but often Tay-nee) which, as one writer aptly observed, "broods in bronze outside the State House portico." Later, we'll talk more about this esteemed jurist—Chief Justice of the U.S. Supreme Court from 1836 until his death in 1864; law partner and brother-in-law of Francis Scott Key; and, less esteemed, deliverer of the Dred Scott opinion, which helped start the Civil War.

It was Taney, who studied law and practiced in Annapolis among many distinguished lawyers and patriots, who gave the city of those years the sobriquet "The Athens of America."

Of course, I knew none of this as a youth sitting on his statue's knee, on the east front at the top of the hill, viewing Church Circle as if I was a king on a bronze throne. Leaning against the statue's green bronzed hand that rested on a bronze book replica entitled *The Constitution*, I was touching history.

As kids, we were always touching history on State House

hill. Near Taney's statue we'd climb an old cannon, riding it like a horse. That cannon was brought from England on March 25, 1634, by Maryland's original settlers and mounted on a fort at their first settlement in St. Mary's City. It was recovered from St. Mary's River in 1822.

A preteen Ralph Crosby on State House Hill by Roger Brooke Taney's statue (top left).

We played hide-and-seek on the hill, often ducking into the alcove entrance to the Old Treasury Building, now the oldest public building in Maryland. A small, brick structure in the shape of a Greek cross, it was completed in 1737 as the office of the commissioners responsible for administration of Maryland's newly authorized paper currency. Eventually it became the Maryland State Treasurer's office, from which it derived the "Old Treasury" name. For us kids, it was a great hiding place, including behind the giant old trees that surrounded it.

On the other side of the State House, the southwest side closer to Main Street, was a sword-wielding statue we could climb on and pretend we were joining him on the battlefield. Into battle he went, fighting for American independence. The monument honors Baron Johann de Kalb, a French Brigadier who, like Lafayette, came over to help Americans fight the Revolutionary War.

In 1780, leading the famous Maryland Line in a battle at Camden, South Carolina, his force of about 600 fought off 2,000 British until he fell, wounded eleven times, and died three days later. After more than 100 years, in 1883, the U.S. Congress approved this statue of him in Annapolis.

From my perch on the de Kalb statue, holding on to a protruding coat of arms on its pedestal, I looked directly at a house with a long front porch on Church Circle, a house I mentioned earlier as an entertainment haven because it was the back of the Elks lodge. While the primary Elks' entry was on Main Street (labeled "BPOE"), the State Circle entrance, with its elk's head replica on the roof, was entrance to the upstairs parlor, location of the lodge's television set, and where my dad and I joyfully watched the Army-Navy football games in the late 1940s before we owned a TV set, experiencing more joy if Navy won. As I sat watching television in that old house on Church Circle, I was unaware that I was sitting in the living room of John Shaw—patriot, distinguished Annapolis cabinetmaker and caretaker of the State House.

Born in Scotland in 1745, Shaw came to Annapolis around 1763 and opened a cabinetmaking shop with a partner on Church Street. At the time, Annapolis was a cabinetmaker's dream, given the luxurious lifestyle of provincial officials stationed in the City and the wealthy tobacco planters building grand Annapolis town houses. In the early 1770s, when Shaw was getting his business moving, at least nine important townhouses were built, requiring much furniture.

For Shaw, an additional opportunity came with his first commission for the State House, a pine bookcase. Shaw became indispensable at the State House, taking on construction and maintenance jobs as well as commissions for furniture, such as mahogany ballot boxes, a mahogany table, desks, stools and a table with pigeonholes for the state auditor's office.

Across from the State House sits the John Shaw House, part of the Elks Club in my youth, when it became a source of recreation for my family.

Known for his patriotic fervor, Shaw was appointed armorer for Maryland in 1777, in charge of stocking arms and ammunition for the Revolutionary army—a position he would hold until 1819. Putting his cabinetmaking skills to war time use, he also made cartridge boxes and packing cases for guns. A soldier, too, Shaw served in the Severn Battalion during the Revolution, reaching the rank of Sergeant Major.

In 1784, Shaw purchased the house on State Circle. Its location directly across from the State House was convenient in carrying out government commissions. (For example, that year, when the Continental Congress convened in Annapolis, Shaw sold a cabinet to Thomas Jefferson.) Shaw continued to work on State House projects into the 1800s. When he passed away in 1829, the local paper, *The Maryland Gazette*, called him "one of the oldest and most respectable inhabitants of this city" who "in the gallant and arduous struggle for our independence, he espoused the cause of freedom…"

About 100 pieces of Shaw's furniture remain extant today,

evidence of his prodigious output as a cabinetmaker. Learning of Shaw's productivity and remarkable life make my hours in his living room an even more satisfying memory of days around State House hill.

Chapter Four

"The Most Historic Room in the Country"

My youthful forays to the State House were not confined to the hill. I often entered the State House itself, seldom being bothered by guards. I always felt a sense of the building's majesty, walking into the broad hall with its black and white checkered stone floors, my footsteps often echoing as sound traveled up the dome, rising 113 feet from the floor.

That spire, topped by a distinctive, 800-pound golden acorn made of cypress, which I viewed often from my front room window on Main Street and even more visible from my back porch, is the largest wooden dome in the country constructed without nails. It sits upon the oldest state capitol still in continuous legislative use. After fire and deterioration destroyed two original state capitols on that site, the first built in 1698 and the second in 1706, the current building was completed in 1779 and a legislature has met there annually ever since.

I can remember climbing the stone steps to the portico, behind four large, white pillars facing the back of the Taney statue, and opening the large entrance door, where immediately on my right was the room that makes the State House such a fantastic historic landmark—a room known as the "Old Senate Chamber."

Historians would probably argue that the most historic room in the U.S. is either Philadelphia's Independence Hall where both the Declaration of Independence and the U.S. Constitution were debated and adopted; or Boston's Faneuil Hall, the patriotic meeting place that presaged the Revolution; or even the White House's Oval Office. But the Old Senate Chamber rivals them in consequence. Admittedly prejudiced, I lean toward the opinion of author Mynna Thruston, writing in 1916 in her book, *A Day in Historic and Beautiful Annapolis*:

"The Old Senate Chamber opened on the right, and when we entered it, we were in the most historic room in the country...."

State House archivists are not so definitive, but call it "one of the most significant rooms in the nation."

There are several reasons for this significance. First, of course, it is the room where George Washington would resign his military commission and return to private life. Second, Congress' final approval of the Treaty of Paris, which formally ended the Revolution, took place in the Old Senate Chamber. Even Thomas Jefferson's after-Revolution assignment as Minister Plenipotentiary to France was approved in that room. And all of this occurred there when Annapolis was capital of the colonies, and with the approval of the Treaty of Paris, became the first capital of an independent United Sates of America and the Maryland State House, its first peacetime capitol.

The Maryland State House's Old Senate Chamber, as it appeared in my youth. One of the most historic rooms in the United States, it is where George Washington resigned his Revolutionary War Commission. (Collection of the Maryland State Archives)

The door to the Old Senate Chamber, open and guarded only by a rope, intrigued me as a youth. By then, I had learned about the heroics and myths of George Washington. I remember sneaking under the rope and, while I don't remember it specifically, I can imagine standing on the bronze plaque that marked the spot where Washington stood to return his commission to Congress and my pretending to be the hero who stood triumphant after the battle of Yorktown in the painting on the wall. (Visiting the Old Senate

Chamber in 2015, after it's restoration to its 1783 appearance, I found a quite different room, with bright, light wooden floors, replica chairs of the period, and a balcony where women would have sat to hear Washington resign, and with a bronze statue of Washington standing on the spot where he would have addressed the president of Congress. Washington's original handwritten speech sits under glass in the rotunda outside the Old Senate Chamber.)

Washington's Resignation

On the morning of December 23, 1783, George Washington arrived at the State House shortly before noon. Leaving his horse on the hill, he entered that portico doorway.

A committee chaired by Thomas Jefferson had scripted the retirement ceremony, and Washington and the 21 congressmen assembled knew their roles.

Precisely at noon, Washington entered the Old Senate Chamber and took his seat before the legislators and the galleries full of Maryland and Annapolis dignitaries, including ladies in the gallery above the entrance door. The congressmen remained seated and kept their hats on, not a sign of disrespect but either a custom from British Parliament or an anti-monarchial gesture symbolizing Congress' authority (in Europe, in the presence of royalty, commoners stood and doffed their hats).

The script decreed that when "the General rises to make his address, and also when he retires, he is to bow to Congress, they are to return by rising and uncovering without bowing." Dutifully, when the General arose to speak he bowed and, in return, the congressmen removed their three-square cocked hats in lieu of a bow, then replaced them.

Washington arose with speech in hand, and contemporary accounts say that hand shook violently, and his voice was hoarse with emotion. The speech took only about three minutes; he ended his military life with, among others, these words:

"Happy in the confirmation of our Independence and sovereignty, and pleased with the opportunity afforded the United States of becoming a respectable nation, I resign with satisfaction the appointment I accepted with diffidence."

When he finished his speech, Washington withdrew from his pocket the document that appointed him Commander in Chief, dated June 15, 1775, and returned it to the presiding officer of the Congress. One witness recalled the scene: "The spectators all wept, and there was hardly a member of Congress who did not drop tears."

A month after the event, in a letter to her mother, Annapolitan Mrs. John Ridout wrote:

"The General seemed so much affected himself that everybody felt for him. He addressed Congress in a short speech, but very affecting. Many tears were shed. He has retired from all public business and desires to spend the rest of his days at his own seat. I think the world never produced a greater man and very few so good."

The latter sentiment was shared by most Americans, and spending the "rest of his days at his own seat" in Virginia was certainly Washington's sentiment. However, in writing his resignation speech, Washington originally called his resignation "final" and "ultimate" retirement from public service. He removed those words, perhaps foreseeing that the country would call on him to lead once more, as it did on April 30, 1789, when he was elected President of the United States.

Following the resignation ceremony, Washington bid goodbye to each member of Congress and, having had his bags packed earlier, he headed for the door and his horse. Accompanied by his friend, Maryland Governor William Paca, a signer of the Declaration of Independence, he headed to the South River Ferry below Annapolis, on route to his beloved Mount Vernon to celebrate Christmas, 1783, with his wife Martha.

Painters who later tried to capture the resignation scene managed glorious portraiture but painted false pictures, including Martha at Washington's side when, actually, she was at Mount Vernon awaiting his arrival.

It was not so much the words of Washington's speech that impacted history, though they certainly were important, but the speech's true significance rests on Washington's moral strength. Historians call it the most critical decision of American history.

During the revolution, Congress had given Washington extraordinary powers and, following his victory, many wanted to make him America's king. But he would have none of it. In his recounting of the resignation, author Stanley Weintraub, in his book, *General Washington's Christmas Farewell*, concluded: "For its implications it was also, however early it occurred in American history, the most significant address ever delivered to a civil society."

A fanciful version of Washington resigning his commission in the Old
Senate Chamber—painted by Edwin White—includes Martha Washington,
who was not present. (Collection of the Maryland Archives)

Thomas Jefferson undoubtedly would have agreed. As Jefferson
wrote to Washington later, "The moderation and virtues of a single
character… probably prevented this revolution from being closed,
as most others have been, by a subversion of that liberty it was
intended to establish."

Even George III, whose British army Washington defeated, is
reported to have said that if the General won the war and returned
to private life, "he will be the greatest man in the world."

Thus in a 30 foot by 40 foot room in the Maryland State House,
the primacy of civilian rule over military power was firmly
established, setting the cornerstone of American democracy. It was
perhaps, the first time in history that a victorious military leader
refused to assume power.

And, history continued to be made in that 30 foot by 40 foot
room.

Treaty of Paris

There's a restaurant in the Maryland Inn called "The Treaty of
Paris," where I have dined often, mainly because it's the only place
serving Yorkshire pudding, those puffy popovers slathered with
butter, much enjoyed in the surrounding 18th century atmosphere.

During my days as a young reporter covering the Maryland

legislature, I would meet at the Inn with fellow journalists and politicos over a scotch and soda, usually one for me and many for them. The legislative discussions there paled in comparison to the talk in the 18th century, especially in the days that gave the restaurant its modern name.

Like a flatiron building, The Maryland Inn sits at the top of Main and Duke of Gloucester Streets. It is home of the Treaty of Paris Restaurant, where politicians have been fed since George Washington's day. (Courtesy of M.E. Warren Photography, LLC)

Seemingly an odd name for a restaurant, "Treaty of Paris" makes sense when you realize that the congressmen who approved the Treaty in the Old Senate Chamber in 1784 celebrated the ratification at the Maryland Inn. They probably had drinks and ate Yorkshire pudding, too, since the latter was a dish of the period.

Those 1784 congressmen must have celebrated with relief. They almost didn't make the ratification deadline.

Following Washington's victory at Yorktown in 1781, the Revolutionary War slowly halted, but hostilities did not cease formally until September 3, 1783, when a treaty document with Great Britain was signed in Paris by American representatives John Adams, Benjamin Franklin and John Jay.

The Treaty stipulated that the American Congress approve and return the document within six months. Ratification required the presence of nine of the thirteen states. Given that it took nearly two months to get a document across the Atlantic, the Congress grew concerned when a sufficient number of delegates had not arrived in Annapolis by mid-December, 1783. Thomas Jefferson lamented, "We have no certain prospect of nine states in Congress and cannot ratify the Treaty with fewer."

Finally, representatives of Connecticut and New Jersey arrived making a quorum, and on January 14, 1784, Congress voted unanimously to approve the Treaty and sent copies off immediately to England and France. The Treaty confirmed British recognition of American independence and, thus, action in the Old Senate Chamber took on even more significance and made Annapolis the new nation's first capital city.

Jefferson in Annapolis

Thomas Jefferson's imprint on American history was felt strongly in Annapolis, especially during the period from November 26, 1783 to August 13, 1784, when the town hosted Congress. He worked in the State House, especially in the Old Senate Chamber, which served as Congress' home at the time.

In preparation for writing this book, I spent some time at the State House to jog my memory of youthful visits there. On one trip I was accompanied by my friend Michael Busch, speaker of the Maryland House of Delegates. A former teacher, Mike taught my children in high school, but we became friendly when we both served as board directors of the Annapolis Touchdown Club.

On our tour, Mike introduced me to then Maryland Lieutenant Governor Anthony Brown, who proudly showed off his office as the one-time office of Thomas Jefferson. While there is no documentation to identify which specific rooms were used by members of the Continental (or Confederation) Congress, legend supports Anthony Brown, for Jefferson did work on the second floor.

During that period, Jefferson was busy in the Old Senate Chamber even beyond helping oversee Washington's resignation and shepherding the approval of the Treaty of Paris. Congress passed his April 23, 1784 Land Ordinance, which created new states out of the land west of the Appalachian Mountains and laid the groundwork for future expansion, which also was one purpose of the Treaty of Paris. The Treaty defined the east-to-west borders of the American colonies from the Atlantic Ocean to the Mississippi River, and its north-south borders from Canada to Spanish Florida.

Even then, Jefferson had his eye on the American west. While in Annapolis he wrote to George Rogers Clark, a Virginia military leader and Revolutionary War hero, about making "an attempt to search that country." Jefferson feared that other countries would try to colonize the frontier beyond America's control. (Under President Jefferson, Clark's younger brother William would co-lead the exploration known as the Lewis and Clark Expedition, which explored the country all the way to the Pacific Ocean.)

The Continental Congress was to put another feather in Jefferson's cap in the Old Senate Chamber in May of 1784, when it added him to its mission to Europe, joining Ben Franklin and John Adams in establishing alliances for the new nation. Thus, in the first such appointment by the new nation, he became a United States diplomat with full powers to deal with foreign governments.

It's ironic that Thomas Jefferson would achieve so much in the Old Senate Chamber. On a trip to New York in 1766, he stopped in Annapolis and, while he found the City "extremely beautiful," he was not impressed with the Maryland legislative chambers.

During the Continental Congress Convention, Jefferson enjoyed living in Annapolis, especially because he shared housing with his good friend James Monroe, a future president, as well. They rented a residence just off Church Circle, literally a stone's throw from St. Anne's Church. Many members of Congress lived on Maryland Avenue during Revolutionary times, leading to its early nickname—"Patriots' Walk." In the 18th Century, Maryland Avenue ran from the State House to the banks of the Severn River, where the Naval Academy would one day arise.

(In my youth, Midshipmen who patronized the many naval tailor shops and other stores on Maryland Avenue, which by then ran from the State House to the Naval Academy's main gate, nicknamed it "Robber's Row.")

After the Revolution, Jefferson would return to Annapolis occasionally. In 1790, he and another president-to-be, James Madison, stopped in Annapolis on their way home to Virginia from New York, and climbed the 149 steps up the State House Dome, from which you could view the whole city then as you can today. You could see the Chesapeake Bay and, on a clear day, the eastern shore across the Bay. The streets of Annapolis would spread before you like the spokes of a wheel, though there would be a second wheel with spreading spokes from nearby St. Anne's Church.

Mike Busch offered me the trip up the dome, but I declined, intimidated by the 149 steps. As we walked from under the dome into the newer section of the State House (added in 1906), I did request a visit down the wide marble stairway with its large balustrades to the lower floor to visit the press rooms where I had worked in the late 1950s.

When I graduated from the School of Journalism at the University of Maryland in 1956, I landed a reporter's job on Hearst's Baltimore *News Post*, a throwback to the "Front Page" kind of old-fashioned newspaper. In 1958, I was assigned to cover the Maryland legislature, as a backup to our regular political reporter, Jim Connolly, who had a habit of disappearing into the various taverns of Annapolis. When Mike escorted me downstairs, I wasn't surprised to find that the press rooms, themselves, hadn't changed in more than half a century, except that computers had replaced the typewriters and the infernal Teletype machine we punched directly to the *News-Post's* Baltimore building.

My college roommate and friend, Hal Burdett, who followed me as a *News-Post* State House reporter, recalls a telltale incident about that Teletype machine and Jim Connolly. Jim was Teletyping a story to the paper when he was interrupted by a message from the home office:

"The machine has periods and commas," the chiding message came from an editor, "why not use them?" So Jim typed out a row of periods and a row of commas and replied, "Here's a bunch of periods and commas; use them where you like."

The young journalists behind their computers who I met when visiting with Mike Busch would not get a taste of old-time journalism that I experienced with Jim Connolly and his hard-drinking ilk. For example, as the "kid" working in Baltimore Saturday nights to put out the Sunday paper, one of my jobs was to make runs to the nearby bar to buy whiskey miniatures for the grizzled old rewrite men on the City desk. Those old-timers taught me a lot about the positives of newspaper writing and the negatives of whiskey drinking.

Passing the Old Senate Chamber to the front door as I was about to leave, Mike Busch looked out the front window at Taney's statue and noted its conflicting implication with the statue that sits at the other end of the State House—that of another Maryland U.S. Supreme Court Justice, Thurgood Marshall, and the historic civil rights disparity they represent, which we'll explore later when we discuss "Annapolis' racial journey."

Ralph Crosby, the journalist, typing at the Baltimore News Post city desk in the late 1950s.

Leaving the State House from the east portico, I was transported back to my teenage years by the sight before me. Then, if you stood on the portico behind Taney's statue, State Circle would reveal historic Francis and Cornhill Streets straight ahead. To the right of Francis Street was the building where my mother worked at the time as a secretary in an insurance company office. Next to that building was Tate Alley, across from our apartment building and only two outstretched arms wide, my usual route to and from Main Street.

Cornhill Street, the home to historic but then decaying row houses where some of my friends lived, went down to Market Space and the nearby Community Market, where I worked my senior year in high school to help defray upcoming college costs. On the left corner at the top of Cornhill Street was the Circle Theater, where my buddies and I spent many an exciting hour watching the likes of John Wayne and Humphrey Bogart defeat the "Japs" and Nazis, and on the right corner was the Tilghman family jewelry store.

Tilghman, Peale and Lafayette

The store's eventual proprietor, my friend Tom Tilghman, with whom I served for 20 years as a director of Annapolis Bank and Trust, descended from the family of Marylander Tench Tilghman, George Washington's aide-de-camp during the Revolutionary War. When Washington defeated British General Lord Charles Cornwallis at the battle of Yorktown, Virginia, effectively ending the war, he sent Lt. Col. Tench Tilghman to deliver the surrender papers to the Continental Congress in Philadelphia. On his way, Tilghman stopped in Annapolis with the official news, giving my forbears a leg up on celebration.

Tench Tilghman remained Washington's friend and adviser after the war, though Tilghman died at age 42 from illness contracted during the Revolution. Evidence of his closeness and importance to Washington can be seen in famous portraitist Charles Willson Peale's painting, now on display in the room next to the Old Senate Chamber, which shows Washington in the aftermath of his Yorktown victory. The Marquis de Lafayette stands between Washington and Tench Tilghman, who clutches the Yorktown articles of capitulation. In a confluence of patriots, it was John Shaw, as caretaker of the State House, who originally hung this painting in the Old Senate Chamber, where I would view it as a youth and let my imagination soar.

Charles Willson Peale, too, had a special connection to Annapolis. He came to the City from the Eastern Shore as a child. Eventually he set up a saddle shop and sign painting business on Church Street (Main Street) in 1762, but his interest was in portraiture. Showing some talent after trading his best saddle for painting lessons from a well-known portraitist, he persuaded a group of affluent men, most from Annapolis, including Charles Carroll the Barrister, to put up the money to send him to England to study painting.

Charles Willson Peale's painting of the victors at Yorktown, with the Marquis de Lafayette standing between George Washington and Marylander Tench Tilghman, who clutches the British articles of Capitulation. In my youth, it hung on the Old Senate Chamber wall. (Collection of the Maryland State Archives)

Returning to Annapolis after more than two years, Peale began his formal career specializing in portraits of Washington, including several as early as 1772, one when Peale visited Mount Vernon and another when the then Virginia Colonel came to Annapolis for Race Week. Peale's involvement with revolutionary patriots (he joined them in opposing the British Crown) led to portraits of Ben Franklin, John Hancock, Alexander Hamilton, Thomas Jefferson and, in 1779, a painting of the Marquis de Lafayette in a hand-in-jacket pose made famous by another and contemporary Frenchman, Napoleon Bonaparte.

Major General Gilbert du Motier, Marquis de Lafayette, volunteered to fight for the Americans' cause against Great Britain and won the confidence of General Washington, who put the young Frenchman—all of 22—in charge of an American regiment, which brought Lafayette to Annapolis.

Leading 1,200 troops to Annapolis in March of 1781, he camped across Spa Creek from the City in an area that is now called Eastport. Lafayette and some of his French officers were wined and dined by Annapolis' leading citizens, and the dashing Frenchmen considerably impressed the ladies of the town.

Lafayette fought the British all the way to Yorktown, then returned to France. He came back in 1784 to say a formal farewell to his troops and to visit his friend George Washington. Washington traveled from Mount Vernon to Annapolis, where officials honored both generals. Maryland officially proclaimed Lafayette "and his male heirs forever... natural born citizens" of Maryland.

Lafayette made one more trip to Annapolis in December of 1824, at the invitation of the Maryland legislature. In response to the invitation, Lafayette wrote that Annapolis was very dear to his heart and that he was bound to the City by many ties. His visit was part of the celebration of the 50th Anniversary of the Declaration of Independence.

In Annapolis, Lafayette, accompanied by his son, George Washington Lafayette, was met with much fanfare, including a 21-gun salute. On a visit to the State House, the then 67-year-old Marquis addressed the crowd in the Old Senate Chamber, recalling with deep sentiment his friend and commander's resignation in that room. (Though after Lafayette's departure in 1784, he and Washington promised by correspondence to meet again, they never did. By the 1824 visit, President Washington had passed on.)

I would cross State House hill and enter the State House myriad times over the years, and the memories of youthful play always came rushing back. Even as an adult, I couldn't look at Taney's statue without an itch to climb it.

As I grew out of my more geographically confined early years, my playgrounds grew more numerous. Though many of these playgrounds were still steeped in history, history had little to do with my interests, which would center on seemingly conflicting pool balls and library books.

Chapter Five

Pool Balls and Library Books

Eventually, having outgrown climbing statues on State House hill, I moved on to other, diverse playgrounds, most notably St. John's College and the U.S. Naval Academy. But, before that, I discovered a greater haven and met my first mentor—both at the same time in the same place. I found them about a block away from 183 Main.

On Church Circle, two street spokes off the wheel around St. Anne's Church—between West and Franklin Streets—stood a building with two signs. One said "Reynolds Tavern;" the other "Public Library."

Historic Reynolds Tavern, built in 1747, became Annapolis' public library and one of my favorite childhood sanctuaries in the 1940s. (Collection of the Maryland State Archives)

Some of the land around Church Circle was originally property of St. Anne's Church—"Glebe Land" used to help pay church expenses. Thus, in 1747, Lot 60 across from the Church was leased to William Reynolds, who built the two-and-one-half story, five bay brick structure as his home and place of business. Originally a hatter, Reynolds turned his well-located home into a tavern and hostelry, though he continued to make hats at the same location.

Originally known by the typically English name, "Beaver and Lac'd Hat," the Tavern stayed in the Reynolds family for many years, acquiring its surname in the process. In the 1800s the building became a banking facility—modified by the illustrious cabinet maker John Shaw. It later served as home for the President of Farmer's National Bank, which had been built next door on the West Street side.

Seeking a better, larger home for a library rather than a few rooms in already occupied public buildings, the local library association acquired Reynolds Tavern from Farmer's National Bank for $20,000 in 1936. In 1937, Miss Esther King, a graduate of Columbia University's Library School, left her job at a Baltimore department store's book department to become the librarian at Reynolds Tavern.

My mother enjoyed reading books of English history—mostly romantic novels about the period—and would make regular trips up the street to acquire and return them at the library. She often took me along, and I would look through children's books in the kids' section at the back of Reynolds Tavern.

It was during those trips that Miss King took a liking to me. Short in stature and pixieish in facial appearance, Miss King wasn't pretty and wasn't homely. She seemed schoolmarmish in appearance but not in attitude. Her ready smile and kind manner made her always approachable. I remember her having a touch of grey in her hair, though in my youth, she wasn't elderly by any means. She had a welcoming way of making you feel at home in the library. No shooshing when you made a little noise. As I grew a bit older, she began to suggest books I might like and would have a few at the ready for what became my consistent trips to the library. It was so convenient. Any trip around Church Circle, which occurred almost daily, meant a stop at the library.

I remember Miss King talking to me about two brothers, Frank and Joe Hardy, who solved mysteries, and thus the Hardy Boys books became a favorite. She knew, like most boys my age, that sports were important, so the exploits of baseball and football stars were waiting for me at her desk in the right hand room when you entered the building. I recall reading *Hans Brinker*, or *The Silver Skates*, the portrait of 19th Century Dutch life, an ice-skating race for the Silver Skates prize, and the side story of the little boy who uses his finger to plug a leak in the dike and save his country. Another favorite of Miss King's, passed on to me, was Zane Grey's *Riders of the Purple Sage*. Each book was just a suggestion from Miss King with not much proselytizing about the value of reading. She was too smart for that; she knew that through exposure I would discover the joys of reading.

Then Miss King sprung on me Mark Twain's book, *The Adventures of Tom Sawyer*, whose main character thrilled me with his mischievous exploits. That was followed by a more exciting and more thought-provoking book by Twain, *Adventures of Huckleberry Finn*. Though as a preteen, the human conflicts in the book probably escaped my conscious mind, they must have had a subconscious impact, for I have returned to the book several times over the years, each time finding some new nugget of wisdom.

Eventually, I made my way up to the second floor—the literature floor—of Reynolds Tavern, where I would sit on its original broad, dark wooden floor boards, reading Tennyson's poems, Hemingway's stories and Emerson's essays, and other writings of their famous literary ilk. There the reading habit and dreams of writing, myself, became ingrained in my life.

In the course of time, I lost track of Miss King. The library moved out of downtown in 1965, and I moved on to college and career, using libraries in Baltimore and Washington, D.C., where I worked. Miss King retired in 1971, having helped build a healthy library system throughout Anne Arundel County. Losing track does not mean losing memories, and I will never forget Miss Esther King and her kindness to the boy from Main Street and her impact on my life, fostering literature and a desire to write.

America's First Public Library

On the subject of local libraries, the modern public library system in Annapolis and Anne Arundel County didn't open until 1920, but that wasn't the first public library in Annapolis. The first one, established in 1696, was the first public library in the American colonies.

The Reverend Thomas Bray, sent to Maryland to represent the Church of England, was commissioned by the Church to establish libraries in the American colonies. While he ultimately founded some fifty libraries in America, his largest collection of books — 1,095 volumes — was deposited in the "Annapolitan Library" between 1696 and 1700.

While the libraries were originally intended for the use of Anglican ministers, the Annapolitan Library was open for public use free of charge. The books were first housed in the almost completed state house building, but when the building burned, the books were moved to King William's School, ultimately St. John's College, where a few of those books still reside. The rest — about 200 remain — are in protected vaults of the Maryland State Archives.

While much of the library's history is fuzzy, Ford K. Brown, in his booklet *The Annapolitan Library at St. John's College*, says despite that, "there are enough available records to make some facts about it clear. It was the first library that Dr. Bray projected, and the first of his collections to be sent to America.... Most important, there is no doubt that it was the first public library in the colonies."

The Pool Room

When I reached age 15, I didn't spend quite as much time at the library because I found another sanctuary, and the sights and sounds it produced have stayed with me forever.

I'll never forget the *clack! clack!* of the balls bouncing in "Pap's." The sound of pool balls colliding as they rolled on the green felt-topped tables was music to my ears as I entered what we called Pap's pool room, literally a stone's throw from 183 Main. While we called it Pap's after one of the business owners, George Pappas, its official name was "Brunswick Billiard Hall." The more business-like name may have been appropriate since it was frequented by the town's politicians, businessmen and working men — yes, it was men only — as well as local gamblers and kids like me enjoying the sport and camaraderie, as well as trying to earn a few dimes.

The pool room was located at 163 Main Street, three storefronts across Conduit Street, on part of the property that had once housed Mann's Tavern. The building had several distinctive characteristics. One was the double arches that decorated the front of the downstairs, surrounding full plate glass windows. Another was the tin ceiling featuring large square panels with bacchanalian figurines, male and female, enjoying glasses of wine. Those figures were the only females in the pool room, except for George Pappas' daughter Helen, who would help out occasionally. Helen, whose sister Frances was my school classmate, would later operate the pool room with her husband, Pete Palaigos, and the pool hall would become known as "Pete's Place."

We were all bound together by neighborhood, as well as commerce, since the Pappases lived on Duke of Gloucester Street and the Palaigoses on Conduit Street. I would often go through the Pappas home's back gate to get from Main Street to Duke of Gloucester.

George Pappas had a partner, his cousin James Fotus, and both figuratively winked when I strode into the pool room at age 15, pretending I was 16, the entry age to their establishment.

I became enamored with the sights, sounds and smells of the pool room at an early age, having entered to find my father who stopped there often. I loved the sound of pool balls clacking and slot machines whirring, mixed with such expressions as: "Great shot!" "Get in the Pocket!" "Damn stick must be crooked!" It also had a unique smell combining odors of beer, shoe shine polish and steam from the hat cleaning compartment, plus so many bodies in motion. I just loved it.

The men only structure was not the only evidence of discrimination of the time. The black rack boys, who doubled as shoe shine boys, became friends of ours inside the pool hall, but that friendship did not extend to the segregated outside world.

We shot eight ball, nine ball and straight pool, almost always for money, for a dime or quarter mostly, but rarely for the "large" sum of one dollar. I couldn't afford that until my later teen years, which worked okay because by then I had become a more proficient shooter.

The cast of characters who frequented the pool room spread across the economic and social strata of Annapolis. I saw the mayor and other elected officials in the pool room; though I never saw them in the library. The same might be said of the town bums. Among my pool-shooting heroes was Beano DiMaggio, perhaps the best shot in Pap's. As good as I became, I wasn't in his league. Beano was father to two of my friends, Mickey and Don DiMaggio, both great athletes but not pool sharks like their dad. The handsome Doc Stevens cut quite a figure with the ladies as well as at the pool table. He was almost as good as Beano and would agree to shoot with me from time to time. Johnny Jarrell, a man in his thirties with a crippled leg but a good pool stroke, would shoot with me despite the age difference. My classmate, Donald Jones, was in Doc Stevens' class as a shooter and would beat me regularly.

A number of regulars were World War II veterans, since the war had raged only five years earlier. One I remember most clearly was Owen Harrison, a friendly guy who would joke around with me and others. Owen, about 10 years older than I, had been a bomber belly or tail gunner during the war, I was told. You'd think he didn't have a care in the world.

Then one really hot summer day in the pool room, Owen took off his shirt to cool down, to reveal a series of round scars down his back where he had been strafed while strapped into his gun turret. That was a lesson in overcoming adversity.

Another day and another lesson I remember from the pool room involved my friend and classmate Roger "Pip" Moyer. Pip and I played basketball together around age nine. A chubby guy, he was slow in running the court. But he could shoot the basketball, so we'd wait until he was in position then feed him the ball to put his scoring ability to work.

Pip came to the pool room one end-of-summer day, and I hardly recognized him. It was as if someone had put Pip's head on a tall, lean body. He had spent the summer losing weight and, boy, did it show in his appearance and his self-image. Pip went on to be a great high school, college and recreation league basketball player. He also went on to be Mayor of Annapolis. He was a good example of what hard work and determination could accomplish.

So, while the library taught me a lot through reading, the pool room taught me a lot by watching human nature at work. It was there I began to realize I was really good at a lot of things, but not great at any one thing. It was true in pool, sports, school and work. It was also there it dawned on me that the harder one worked the "gooder" one got. Practicing specific pool shots over and over, I discovered I could make them more and more.

These pool room lessons were to help immensely in my careers as a journalist and marketer. I had to outwork the next guy in order to succeed.

In addition to the pool tables, Pap's provided its patrons with refreshments, both sartorial and whistle-whetting. As you entered the pool room, a hat cleaning and blocking cubbyhole was on your left, important in those days when men wore hats daily and cleaning and shaping well-worn and dirty fedoras was necessary. The cubbyhole was followed by a high shoe shine bench that could seat several patrons. Across from the shoe shine stand was a long stand-up bar where beer, soft drinks and a few snacks satisfied thirsty patrons. A small bench sat at the end of the bar which, along with the end seat on the shoe shine stand, overlooked the first pool table, unofficially reserved for the best shooters. By 18 years old, I was good enough to challenge some of the good shooters on the first table.

Like many working men of the day, my dad would stop at the pool room on his walk home from work at the Naval Academy to have a ten-cent glass of beer before dinner. On those few occasions when I was shooting pool on the first table when dad came in, he would watch. I'd try extra hard to win when he was watching. It was more than ego. Winning on the first table was for my dad a sign of manliness.

So, for a boy who loved books and aspired to be a writer, it was a chance to bond with a man limited by a fifth grade education. Don't get me wrong. I do not demean my dad for his lack of education. I admire him for the reason behind it.

The reason that dad left school at age eleven was the debilitating illness of his father, Richard Eldridge Crosby. My grandfather, a onetime farm boy who worked as a fireman at the Naval Academy, was struck down with what my dad told me was the flu, which could be devastating in those days. I couldn't find a flu epidemic at that precise time, 1912, though there were several before and after. It certainly could have been the flu, but it also could have been typhoid fever, which was spreading along the East Coast at that time. In fact, there was a typhoid outbreak at the Naval Academy in 1910.

Whichever bug it was, it crippled my grandfather, making it difficult to walk. Plus, in a high fever and unconscious at one point in his illness, I was told, a nurse put an ice bag on his forehead and left him alone. The bag slid over his left eye and froze it, blinding him in that eye.

I often passed my grandfather, as I headed down Main Street. He'd be sitting on a stool in front of 165 Main Street, where he and my grandmother lived, also in a third-floor walkup, with two of their nine children still at home. The apartment building at 165 Main also was built on the Mann's Tavern land, next door to the pool room.

The close proximity of family dwellings was pretty normal in a small town like Annapolis. At one point in my childhood, dad's younger brother, Albert, and his family also lived in a Main Street apartment.

When I passed him on his stool, my taciturn grandfather would greet me with little more than a "Hello. How you doing?" I didn't think about it then but what great difficulty it must have been for him to navigate those apartment stairs just so he could watch the happenings on Main Street.

My paternal grandparents, Richard and Sarah Crosby, lived just down the street from our Main Street apartment.

With his father crippled and unable to work, my dad, the oldest child in a then family of seven, quit school to help sustain the family financially. From mentions made by family members—not directly from my dad—I pieced together the jobs he undertook. First he would wake early to work on a milk truck, delivering to homes all over Annapolis. Then, he would go to work delivering ice to homes and restaurants during the day. In those days of little refrigeration, ice was a prime commodity.

In the decade following his leaving school three more children were added to the Crosby family, and my dad would become apprenticed at Wilson's Tin Shop on Main Street, where they made tin roofs, rain spouts and stove pipes. Even then, he worked early morning shifts delivering ice or milk.

By age 21, dad was employed at the Naval Academy's sheet metal shop, always supporting the growing Crosby family. When his sister Catherine died of what they then called "galloping consumption," a virulent case of tuberculosis, her son, my cousin, Daniel Vester Bowser, became part of the family, to be raised by our grandmother, adding one more mouth to feed.

My dad was 30 years old when he married my mother. By then the older Crosby children were on their own.

My dad never shirked from hard work, though he didn't want to manage people. When they made him boss of the Academy's metal shop, and moved him to an office outside of the immediate Academy grounds, he couldn't wait to retire, which he did at the early age of 56 after 35 years on the job. He probably would have stayed longer if they had just left him to do his work as a metal mechanic, walking to and from work with friends and stopping for his beer before dinner. One of my fond memories when Dad stopped at Pap's after work, especially if I was winning at pool, was of buying him his ten-cent draft beer.

Immediately after he retired, dad went to work at the parking lot on Conduit Street. He had no people to manage, just collected money from parkers. It's telling how much neighborhood influenced our lives. Dad's little parking attendant's booth sat on property that had been part of Mann's Tavern. It was behind the apartment where I slept as a baby, behind the Main Street apartment he lived with his parents, behind the pool room and across the street from the alley that went behind what had been the Carroll Barrister House. That alley led to our apartment's back stairway, at the top of which was our kitchen door and my place of childhood discovery, the back porch.

CHAPTER SIX

THE BACK PORCH

When we moved to Main Street, my parents must have been concerned about the safety of their rambunctious four-year-old, living three floors above the street. My dad built an addition of boards on top of the back porch railing so I couldn't fall over. (He also nailed chicken wire to the back of my bedroom window, so I couldn't climb the radiator and fall out an open window.) The back porch was the center of a special universe for an only child with no early childhood playmates. Probably like other only children at that early age I built imaginary worlds. I even had an imaginary friend that I said lived under my bed. My mother supported my fantasy by always asking how he was doing. We called him "Joe Shlump the Midget." I would say goodnight to my imaginary friend and to Ferdinand, the rubber bull on my dresser. "The story of Ferdinand," the tale of a bull who would rather smell flowers than battle in bull fights, was a book turned into a Disney short animated film that was popular in 1938.

The back porch fueled my imagination, but it was full of real experiences. That 12 foot by 20 foot space gave me a different view of the world than the front room windows. For one thing, it overlooked a secret garden. Below the porch, on the left side, hidden from the surrounding activity on Main and Conduit Streets, was the decaying but one-time lush garden of the Carroll Barrister House, with fruits for the picking. I climbed its fading fence to gather grapes and apples and pretend I had entered a foreign land.

My invasions of the Carroll Barrister House gardens went unchallenged by its owner, Mary Davis, though she sometimes watched from her windows. Forbearance must have been a family trait since her relative, our second floor landlord Arthur T. Elliott and his wife Mary, treated me more like a nephew than a tenant's child, despite my rambunctious antics on the back porch and behind the apartment. That's understandable since the Elliotts were childless, and they watched me grow up from age four.

On the side of the porch opposite the garden, I could view the majestic dome of the State House across the roof of the one story stationery store owned by the Jenkins family. Beyond the Jenkins' Stationery Company roof was the Republic Movie House building with an apartment on the top floor occupied by the manager of the Annapolis movie theaters, Lou Schmearman. The Schmearmans also had a back porch, so we were waving neighbors.

Being neighborly, Mr. Schmearman gave me a job as an usher at the Republic when I was a teenager. I repaid him by getting into an argument with my cousin Douglas Crosby, also an usher, while we were filling the candy machine. A few angry words turned into a few thrown candy boxes, witnessed by other staff members. Mr. Schmearman was very apologetic to my mother when he fired me—and cousin Doug—especially since, besides being a neighbor, she also had worked for him as a ticket salesperson.

Being an usher in one of my favorite haunts seemed a glorious opportunity, watching movies while you worked. But the truth is those movies got pretty boring the third, fourth and fifth time around.

I must have had a dozen jobs as a youth, but none of them were more than two or three blocks from 183 Main, one of the benefits of small town living.

Below the back porch was what I called my "back yard," in reality a parking area mostly of stone and dirt in the back of surrounding stores on Conduit and Main. Yet it was an oasis for me. In the back yard, I watched "business" take place.

In my youngest days, William Childs' grocery occupied the main Conduit Street storefront with its rear in the "back yard." My most vivid memory of that time was when Childs' grocers butchered chickens in the yard as I watched from the porch, and the headless birds literally reacted "like chickens with their heads cut off," hopping around madly for several minutes after decapitation.

While it is difficult to believe now, our family's first encounter with pre-sliced bread occurred on the back porch when Childs grocery was part of a Wonder Bread promotion in the late 1930s. Mom picked up a mini-loaf Childs was giving away and we ate sandwiches on the porch. Although the Wonder Company started marketing sliced bread in 1930, apparently it took its time getting to Annapolis.

When I was older, Childs' grocery moved to Main Street, and the Conduit Street store was replaced by E.J. Kramer's slot machine business. Slot machines were legal in Anne Arundel County at the time. The store was filled with machines in various stages of repair, and the back room into which I often got a peek, was used for counting the nickels E.J.'s runners picked up from the various stores and restaurants using the Kramer machines. In places such as the pool room and the Wardroom Restaurant, I often witnessed the runners taking the nickels from the machines and splitting the take with the shop's operator, carrying Kramer's take back to nearby Conduit Street. Whether all the nickels reached Conduit Street was always a question.

From our apartment you got to the back yard down the back steps, past the Elliott's kitchen and back porch that mirrored ours, to the ground floor where the door to the cellar sat on one side and the Elliott's garage door on the other. There was a car in the garage, but I never saw the Elliotts drive it. Like the rest of us, they could walk anywhere they wanted to go. Below the steps on the ground floor was a space I used for hiding things. I kept my bike there and hid my cigarettes there when I started smoking at age 15. The cellar, lit by only one bulb, was full of sounds of the running furnace and creaking water pipes. When I was a grade schooler, I had a child's fearful fantasy of a bogeyman hiding in the cellar and cringed when dad asked me to fetch something from its dungeon-evoking darkness.

When you left the back door you faced the Carroll Barrister garden fence and a cement walk to the back yard, with a patch of dirt where I would try to grow a Victory Garden during World War II. I remember distinctly the stone slab that led from the walkway into the back yard as the place I realized that I would not live forever. Don't ask me why, but I recall the shock of that recognition. Perhaps the slab reminded me of a grave. But I do have a memory of looking at the sky and wondering "Does God exist?" "What will happen when I die?" It was a stunning moment that has stayed with me ever since.

The back yard offered lots of play. I could climb the telephone pole and swing on the "monkey vine" tree in the back of the house that faced Duke of Gloucester Street. The yard had Kramer's back brick wall against which I learned to throw and catch a lacrosse ball and hit a tennis ball—with some accuracy since the wall had two first floor windows about 15 feet apart. It's amazing that I never broke either one. It's also amazing that neither Mr. Kramer nor his staff ever complained about the loud thumping of balls against the wall, especially when they were counting nickels. The yard had enough clear dirt to practice my skills at marble shooting, the main grammar school sport of the time.

I coveted my marble collection and hated to lose any of them in a shootout with another boy. "Back yard" practice made me a reasonably good shooter, especially using my "steely," a steel ball bearing, as my shooter, trying to knock the opponents' marble out of the circle we drew in the dirt, and keeping his marbles as a reward if we were playing "keepers." As much as anything I enjoyed the different sizes and variegated colors of the marbles and the fact that I could enjoy playing marbles by myself.

Of course the marble collection, like the stamp and baseball card collections that would follow, disappeared as childhood moved toward manhood. Somewhat sadly, as the Bible says, "When I was a child, I spoke as a child, I understood as a child, I thought as a child; but when I became a man, I put away childish things."

The alley that led to Conduit Street, which ran past E.J. Kramer's shop, was covered by an apartment above, which would bring me some grief when my dad asked me to help fix its roof. It was a steaming hot Maryland August weekend when we climbed to the roof and my dad lit a fire under the tar we would use to patch the roof. The hot sun, the boiling tar with its acrid odor and the rivers of sweat pouring down my body convinced me, then and there, not to follow my father into metal working or any other manual job.

The alley to Conduit was plastered annually with colorful Barnum & Bailey Circus posters, depicting roaring lions and tigers and the whip wielding trainer announcing the circus was coming to town, which leads me to P.T. Barnum's frightening experience in Annapolis. (Phineas T. Barnum first brought his circus to Annapolis in 1836. His then partner, Aaron Turner, played a trick on the 25-year-old Phineas, telling a crowd of bar patrons that Barnum was Reverend Ephraim Avery, disgraced though acquitted of the hanging murder of a young lady in Rhode Island. Calling Barnum a murderer, more than 100 citizens roughed up P.T. and threatened him with tar and feathers or, worse, lynching, until Turner stepped in to admit the hoax as a joke. When Barnum confronted his partner for playing such a cruel trick, Turner promised it would be good for business and, indeed, Annapolitans filled the circus tent that trip.)

The back porch was our family refuge in hot summer when the rising heat in the third floor became almost unbearable. We never had air conditioning, though I had a small electric fan to bathe me in cool air and whir me to sleep. We would gather on the porch in the cooler evening, and I recall with great fondness my mom and I playing word games and singing some of her old favorites, such as "You Are My Sunshine" and "Nobody's Darlin' But Mine." I'll never forget the first verse of that dirge, for I had the feeling that my mother was singing it to me:

Come sit by my side little darlin'
Come lay your cool hand on my brow
Promise that you will always
Be nobody's darlin' but mine.

The singing really didn't matter; the togetherness did, even for my non-singing dad. Our singing in summer was often drowned out by the loud roar of the Republic Theater's air handler, which pumped air conditioning into the movie house. This huge silver machine sat on the side of the theater overlooking the back yard behind Jenkins'. Air conditioning was something we only enjoyed in movie theaters and some upscale shops. In the 1930s, air conditioning graced few if any Annapolis homes.

The back porch was also a center of housekeeping activity. Mom used the porch to hang out the wash on clotheslines strung from one end to the other. There, in good weather, she set up her curtain stretcher, a wooden frame with tiny nails protruding from the edges, to stretch and dry her crocheted tablecloths and armrest doilies. My dad used the porch for messy jobs, such as mixing paint. I shined my shoes there, and it was my job to sweep it up occasionally. With little extra space in the apartment, my dad built a larger metal container, which he mounted on the porch ceiling, to store my sports equipment—most of which he got for me at the Naval Academy, trading metal work for bats and balls.

It was on the porch also that my mother and I stood when the local firemen came to the back yard to admonish her to punish me for setting a fire to cardboard boxes on the side of Peerless Clothing store on Conduit Street. It wasn't my first experience starting a fire. At about age five or six, while in my bedroom early one morning playing with my parents' matches, I dropped a lighted one in a large cardboard box containing my toys, which sat in the corner of my room. When the contents began to burn, I hastily filled a glass with water in the bathroom next door and poured it on the simmering fire. I repeated that childish reaction several times until—luckily—the fire went out. Only then did I wake my parents. I don't remember their reaction to that, but the Peerless incident also created a reaction—a well-deserved spanking from my mother. Fear of the firemen and punishment from my mom ended my pyromaniac days at age seven. It's hard to imagine such a neighborly firemen-to-family scene today.

The back porch taught me lessons beyond the punishment of pyromania. If it was a bit past 5 p.m., the witching hour for dinner, and I wasn't home, my mother would go to the back porch and yell my name at the top of her voice—like a battlefield call of "Charge!," and I reacted as the soldiers would, instantly moving into action in the race for home.

Because our back porch sat above most of the buildings nearby, my mother's call could be heard for blocks, quite embarrassing at times such as the seventh grade ball game at the grammar school field when mom' s clarion call to dinner forced me to leave mid-game, for which I not only suffered embarrassment but removal from the team.

While that embarrassment and punishment was difficult for me as a youngster, its intent—dinner together as a family—had equally lasting lessons. I can count on one hand the times I have been late for an appointment, and I seldom missed a dinner with my own family.

Those school days gave me the freedom to leave the back porch and the back yard to explore Annapolis, and I discovered its vast opportunities.

Chapter Seven

From Water-Born to Waterborne

O nce I was able to explore Annapolis on my own, I discovered its greatest asset and my greatest childhood recreation—the waterfront. A Baltimore uncle of mine used to say of Annapolis, "If you walk a block in any direction, you fall overboard." A slight exaggeration—but only slight.

Annapolis in my youth was bounded on three sides by water, the Severn River and two of its tributaries, Spa Creek and College Creek, giving the small town more than eighteen miles of shoreline. The Severn and its tributaries offered me unlimited swimming, fishing, ice skating and boating opportunities, extraordinary enjoyment for a small-town, downtown youngster.

Boats, of course, helped create Annapolis. Ships had come up the Bay to the mouth of the Severn as early as 1608, when the famous Captain John Smith ran aground off Greenbury Point. John Smith indicated that the warlike Susquehannock Indians claimed the whole Severn River area as their hunting grounds. Discovery of arrow heads there indicates the presence of humans thousands of years ago.

Sometime after 1649, some settlers from Virginia who sailed up the Chesapeake Bay to select a new home site in Maryland first settled on Greenbury Point at the mouth of the Severn (where the Navy's radio towers would one day be built) and named their settlement "Providence."

Seeking fertile land for tobacco cultivation, some immigrants settled across the Severn on a site on Spa Creek with a deep harbor sheltered by Greenbury Point and Horn Point on land that became Annapolis. Horn Point, with its sand beach and shallow water entry was special to me in my youth. It offered a cool respite from the summer heat and a chance to bond with my dad. Dad would walk me to the neighborhood called Eastport, across the Spa Creek Bridge, a creaky, flat, wooden structure that had to be opened with a hand crank to let sailboats through.

My mom would often join us on our trek to Horn Point,

bringing sandwiches for a picnic, which greatly enhanced the fun of building sand castles and swimming. I learned to swim at Horn Point, where the shallow waters off the sandy beach made it easy to stand up if I floundered. There were sandbars off into the water, some reaching as far as 100 yards, where I could wade out and still only be submerged chest high. On one of those sandbars, George Washington's boat ran aground on his last trip to Annapolis. The President was rescued by his old friend George Mann, who took Washington to his Church Street tavern.

Swimming where Washington was stranded and having him return to stay at the inn that stood on the apartment site where I would later live as a toddler, gives the stuck-on-the-sandbar story special significance for me.

Horn Point was historic beyond the sandbar incident. Because of its strategic location at the water entrance to Annapolis, Horn Point was one of several fort sites built to defend the harbor during the Revolution.

Built in 1776, the fort was constructed with earthen ramparts, trenches for hidden movement and emplacements for fifteen cannons. In 1781 when the Marquis de Lafayette was stationed in Annapolis, his troops manned the fort. Lafayette's troops camped some distance from the fort on a farm at the Eastport end of what became the Spa Creek Bridge.

The old Horn Point Fort was manned again in the war of 1812 against attack by the British, an attack that never came. Knowing American officials expected an attack there, the British bypassed Annapolis and the American forces assembled there and went a different route to burn Washington and the White House.

During the Civil War, Horn Point was site of a hospital for union soldiers recovering from smallpox.

On a research visit to renew my memories of Horn Point, I found a small sandy spot, much shrunken from the expansive beach where I once swam, now labeled "Horn Point Street End Park." In addition to the spot of sand, my memory was jogged by the smell of the Bay, salty and tangy to the nose and deliciously wave-lapping to the ears.

For the eyes, looking toward Greenbury Point, the panorama of the Bay stretching to the Eastern Shore, easily visible on this clear day, was enhanced by a sailboat gliding by, backed by the towers of North Severn, three of which still remain. However, the once open view of the Naval Academy now is obscured by the buildings and boats of waterfront condominiums.

The harbor and the ships that used it defined the commerce that made Annapolis a famous port city. Those ships carried the region's tobacco crop—especially the prized "Golden Orinoco" tobacco—to Europe, along with foodstuffs and building materials. Goods returning to Annapolis included rum, molasses and sugar from the Caribbean; wine from France; spices from the Orient; and tea and manufactured goods from Great Britain. Sadly, some of those ships also brought slaves to Annapolis.

In my youth, many of the boats plying local waters were built in Annapolis, especially across Spa Creek in Eastport. Boatyards lined the shore from Horn Point almost to the headwaters of Spa Creek, a one mile stretch of shoreline that produced some of the world's most famous wooden boats. These boatyards opened to build and service such Chesapeake Bay workboats as the skipjack.

But, as explained in some detail by Rosemary F. Williams in her book, *Maritime Annapolis*, these local shipbuilders reached their zenith in wartime.

Eastport shipbuilders first drew national attention in World War I, when Chance Marine Construction Company, located across Spa Creek from the Naval Academy, built a number of Swift Submarine Chasers, 110 foot wooden vessels that could reach 25 miles per hour.

Chance Marine became Annapolis Yacht Yard and, during World War II, built the British Vosper Patrol Torpedo (PT) boats, built similar PTs for the Russian Navy and manufactured several wooden submarine chasers for the U.S. Navy. After the war, the Annapolis Yacht Yard property was purchased by yacht designer John Trumpy, who developed a yacht-building empire in Eastport. Besides its renowned luxury yachts, Trumpy and Sons built minesweepers during the Korean War and speed patrol boats during the Cold War.

As Rosemary Williams concluded, "These were important years for the boatyards in Annapolis. Government contracts kept the maritime trade alive and thriving, and the town contributed significantly to the efforts in numerous wars and conflicts."

Family Matters

Shipping the cash crop tobacco brought the Crosby progenitor to the area in the 1700s. A sea captain, Burden Crosby undoubtedly sailed out of Annapolis since he was a tobacco transporter. His male line of progeny lived the history of the country and eventually led to the present day descendant—me. My surety of Burden Crosby's voyages carrying tobacco from Annapolis was the event that established Annapolis' place as a maritime leader prior to the Revolution. In 1683, Annapolis was designated an official "Port of Entry," which required that all trade coming or leaving the Maryland province to pass through the City. I wonder if Burden Crosby looked like my father or grandfather and if, on his sea voyage to Annapolis, did he come ashore and walk up Church Street past what would become 183 Main? I would like to imagine that link existed across eight generations.

Under the heading, "The Crosby Family," the book *Colonial Families of Anne Arundel County, Maryland*, by Robert Barnes, states that, "Burden (or Burton) Crosby is the first known ancestor (in America). He was in AA Co. and d. (died) by 25 Jan 1734/5. He m. (married) Elizabeth, dau. of Josias Towgood."

In support of this ancestry, Barnes' book states that Burden Crosby witnessed several deeds in 1732. In one deed he was described as "commander of *The George*," transporting tobacco to London.

My research corroborates that a ship *The George* sailed local waters in those years, though its commander is not mentioned.

Most Crosbys came to America from England and most of those from Liverpool. "Crosby" is a habitational name from various places in southwestern Scotland and northern England and is derived from the Old Norse word "kross" for cross plus "byr," meaning farm or settlement. We do know that Burden Crosby died in England but had a will leaving his Maryland property to his wife Elizabeth. Burden and Elizabeth had two sons, Josias and Richard. Only Josias survived into the 1780s, and it is his line that leads to me. As the bible talks of how a biblical father "begat" a son, so Josias begat John Crosby, born about 1760; who begat Richard Crosby, born 1790; who begat another Richard Crosby, born in 1833; who begat Richard Eldridge Crosby, my grandfather, born 1878; who begat my father. (Josias' son John and his brother Burton, the latter apparently named after the progenitor, were active in the American Revolution. John signed the Oath of Allegiance, required of every free male 18 years or older. By this oath, he renounced the King of England and pledged allegiance to the Revolutionary government of Maryland. Those already engaged in military service, such as John's brother Burton, were assumed to be loyal.)

The oldest of nine children, my dad, Raymond Thomas Crosby, was born in 1901. His friends all called him "Hinky" and when

I'd meet them for the first time, they unfailingly said, "Oh, you're Hinky's boy." My dad claimed he didn't know where the nickname originated, though we speculated that it came from the World War I song, "Hinky, Dinky, Parlez Vous," also known as "Mademoiselle from Armentieres."

Sometimes sung with risqué lyrics, the song was reborn in the Second World War. Why it would create a nickname for my father, we'll never know. One of my cherished possessions is one of my father's hammers with the name "Hinky" burned into the wooden handle.

My mother, born Lillian Sylvia Wolf, suspected her first name was popular because of the famous late 19th and early 20th century actress and singer Lillian Russell. Since my mother was born in 1912 and Lillian Russell was still performing then, it's plausible. But more likely, mom was named after an aunt in New York named Lillian Wolf Mendelberg.

I was named for my grandfather, Raphael Wolf, though, much to my lifelong regret, it was Anglicized to Ralph, a name that neither pleased me nor fit me. I would have preferred Raphael.

Speaking of Anglicizing names, the origin of the family's name "Wolf" is right out of immigration tradition. The story goes that one of the family's early immigrants, from Riga, Latvia, got the name "Thomas Wolf" when an immigration official could not spell either his given name or family name, which was "Tuvah ben Raphael Soloveitchik." Thomas Wolf, nee Soloveitchik, was my great-grandfather and passed one of his original names to his son, my grandfather Raphael. Soloveitchik means "nightingale," quite a variance from "Wolf." My maternal grandmother's maiden name was Molly Frommer, and I was told she emigrated from Russia.

My grandmother Crosby, named Sarah but called "Girlie," while somewhat overweight in my memory, must have been very pretty as a girl. Her daughters were all very good looking and kept young men buzzing around the Crosby household. My grandmother, more than once told me, "You're a good looking boy, but that's natural. There never was an ugly Crosby." Her prejudice aside, my dad was a good looking guy—not Hollywood handsome, but ruggedly attractive, though only 5 foot 8 inches tall. He was square-jawed and trim as a young man with almost perfect, straight white teeth. His teeth were so flawless, in fact, that in his late fifties, when he had his infected tonsils removed, a nurse asked him to remove his false teeth before surgery. He always credited his strong teeth to chewing tar as a youngster. (Chewing tar was an accepted replacement for gum for the poor in the early 20th century up to the depression years, but I doubt if it helped my dad's teeth.)

Not a beautiful woman, my mom is what you would call striking, tall for a woman then at 5 foot 8 inches, the same height as my father, she had clear, almost white skin with lush, wavy, coal black hair that drew compliments. Her features were fine except for the distinctive so-called "Semitic" nose, which was a Wolf family characteristic. In looks, I took after my father, though I grew to six feet tall.

The Crosby family, dad, mom and me, in 1956, the year I graduated from college.

Though a mismatch for many reasons—age, religion, culture—I can see why my parents were attracted to each other. Not only was my dad a good looking, fit and fun-loving man of some experience approaching 30 when he met my mother, he must have seemed a romantic man of the world to an 18-year-old, sheltered girl. Plus, he had a steady job, quite attractive during the depression. Undoubtedly he represented security and freedom from a somewhat bleak oppressive household, darkened by my grandfather Wolf's suicide a few years earlier. Ten older brothers watching over her and her one sister didn't make it any easier. On the other side, my dad had sown his wild oats and a young, vivacious girl probably seemed an attractive choice for settling down.

My Wolf grandparents and their still growing family, c. 1914, with my mother front and center. My Uncle Jerry, baby of the family, hadn't yet been born.

Seafood Bounty

From Burden Crosby's times until the period of my youth, sailing craft were used to transport seafood, mainly oysters and crabs to and from Annapolis. Crabs and oysters, the latter likely introduced to Annapolis settlers by the Indians, were considered inferior food until the mid-1800s. Then both seafoods became so popular that by the 1870s, more than a dozen oysters and seafood houses operated in Annapolis, with the City Dock as the center of the action. Oysters were called "Chesapeake Gold," and in the 19th Century thousands of skipjack sailboats dredged millions of bushels of oysters from the bottom of the Bay. The skipjack, the official boat of Maryland, became the harvester of choice because by law oysters could be dredged only by sailboat until 1965, when the law was amended to allow the use of motorized craft two days a week.

The original of the name "Skipjack" is fuzzy, but old, local watermen believe it derives from the bluefish, plentiful in the Chesapeake Bay, which sometimes seems to skip across the water's surface. In the early 1900s, as many as 20,000 of these sailboats were operating in the Bay to feed the nation's insatiable desire for oysters. At that time, there were oyster beds as close to Annapolis as in the Severn River, but eventually the river was fished out and closed to commercial fishing/oystering above Horn and Greenbury Points. In the 1800s, the City Dock, as the center of the Chesapeake oyster industry, was surrounded by piles of oyster shells as high as the packing houses that shucked and packed the oysters.

Even in my youth, the skipjacks were bringing tons of oysters to Annapolis and these rugged boats sometimes filled the City Dock like a flock of geese landing on a tiny corn field. But the catch has steadily declined since, and with it the skipjack fleet. Some of the remaining few dozen are used for education or as tourist attractions, though a few still ply their oystering trade on the bay. When I was growing up, crabbing provided Annapolis locals both recreation and pocket money as the crabs migrated up the Severn from the Bay. In the late 1940s you could find youngsters and adults crabbing from row boats, piers and shore lines in the Severn and its creeks. Professional watermen, on the other hand, harvested hard crabs using long lines, called "trot lines," baited with salt eels at intervals on the lines, and through fish-bated mesh traps. Friends of mine with piers on their property even had mesh or wooden traps at the end of the pier.

I did my crabbing off of city piers mostly, but some private ones as well, such as the one behind St. Mary's Church and the colonial home of Charles Carroll of Carrollton. The exception was one summer, after a heavy storm, while swimming off Market Street, I saw a row boat bouncing down Spa Creek shorn of any markings or oars. I claimed it, and for a few months, I had my very own boat for crabbing.

You could tell the boat had been painted a battleship grey, but the color was all mottled and streaky, reminding me of aged driftwood, which in a sense, it was. I found some old oars and metal oar locks, and I spent the summer rowing to the best crabbing spots on Spa Creek, proud owner of my own boat. I had no place to keep it so I tied it up at the end of Market Street and, eventually, it left the way it came, gone one day, either adrift or stolen away. But for that short time as a boat "owner," I enjoyed the thrill of ownership—and I caught a lot of crabs.

With my crabbing bait, usually fish heads, plus a ball of twine and a crab net, I'd head for a Spa Creek pier or my boat, tie six or seven lines to the side of the pier or boat—with a metal nut or bolt as a sinker—and wait for the crabs to bite.

The excitement of seeing a line suddenly tighten when a crab latched onto the bait was only exceeded by the thrilling attempt at a catch. Slowly but steadily, you'd pull the line in hand-over-hand until the eating crab appeared below the surface. Then, holding the line with one hand, you'd dip the crab net in the water a distance away from the crab and slowly position the net under the crab. With the stealth of a hunter, but with speed enough to grab the quickly escaping crab, you'd pull the net aboard.

Getting the entangled crab out of the net was a careful act because the crab's claws could do some painful damage to fingers. You had to catch the crab behind its back fin so you could avoid the pinching claws. I'd catch a bushel or more of crabs in the morning and hawk them door-to-door for fifty cents a dozen.

I got my fish heads for crabbing from the trash cans of fish-cleaning waste behind Chesapeake Seafood Company, a packing house on the Naval Academy side of the City Dock, braving the awful smell for free bait. Or, I'd get some meat scraps from Basil's Meat Market on Main Street, where one of the Basil ladies, known as "Pinky," was a close friend of my mother's, giving me an "in" with the butchers. I avoided chicken necks because you usually had to pay for them.

The city dock crowded with work boats that would deliver their catch to buyers such as Chesapeake Seafood, shown in the background, where I "secured" my crab bait. (Courtesy of M.E. Warren Photography, LLC)

Chesapeake Seafood Company was a modern seafood house in those days compared to the fish houses that preceded it. In conversations with my friend and native Annapolitan Lester Trott in 2014, when he was 97 years old, he recalled the wooden fish house that hung over the head of the City Dock in his youth. The shack hung over the water for a purpose; first, to make it easy to buy seafood from the watermen right off their boats, and second, to make it easy to dispose of seafood waste by just throwing it in the water — thus the stench surrounding the dock area.

Lester Trott, who touted Maryland and its seafood officially and unofficially most of his life, recalled working on fishing boats in the Bay during the depression eight to 10 hours a day for $10 a week.

Chesapeake Seafood's location would impact my adult life, as well, because it became the parking lot that drew my friend George Phillips to open his restaurant, the Harbour House, overlooking the same dock area and drew me away from journalism to business and marketing.

We also fished in summer, but you normally needed to be in the Bay to catch the big fish — bluefish and the striped bass, called "rockfish" locally. We mostly caught yellow perch, which required a couple to make a meal, and small colorful sun fish, which we threw back into the water.

I mostly sold my crab catch because my mother was squeamish about cooking them. If I'd catch soft crabs, which develop from the hard crab in a shell molting process, I could sell them for twenty-five cents apiece. Harder to catch because they hid in sea grasses as their shells hardened, the soft crabs became a delicacy in restaurants. My mother's aversion to cooking crabs was not unusual. Some people couldn't stand hearing the hard crabs jump in the boiling pot, scraping the sides as they cooked, and the soft crabs had to have their eyes, mouths and lungs cut out before they were fried. Nor did she like cooking squirrel or rabbit, even though they were skinned and cleaned by my father's friends who gave the animals to him. She said they looked like babies, but I think she feared diseased animals. So in this one case, dad became the cook. My mom wouldn't let me eat these "wild" animals for fear of those unknown diseases. As a result, I tasted neither, though my dad relished them.

Some folks crabbed around the City Dock, where crabs were plentiful (when the boats weren't running) because of the seafood offal thrown in the water by surrounding seafood houses. My earliest memories of the City Dock, when I was nearby in grammar school—long before it became a world-renowned yachting center and tourist attraction—was as a malodorous mess.

Despite the mess, the City Dock was commerce central for many Annapolitans, especially the watermen who sold their catch and often harbored there. The bars and restaurants that surrounded the dock were their social and entertainment centers and drew locals, such as my family, as well. The dock also was a de facto farmer's market. I remember the farmers setting up trucks around the dock selling fresh fruit and vegetables and the old, black lady hawking her delicious crab cakes on crackers.

The offensive odors and polluted harbor spawned a neighborhood beyond the dock called "Hell Point." As I grew older, to have your origins as a "Hell Pointer" became something of a badge of honor. But in my youth being from Hell Point was akin to being "from the other side of the tracks," typical of many 1930s towns, but atypical because no other town had the U.S. Naval Academy next door on "the other side of the tracks."

Chapter Eight

Living With the Four Signers

My greatest Christmas as a youngster was in 1946, when I was thirteen. Gathered with my mom and dad in the front room, I opened several boxes under the tree—only to find a sweater, shirt, and some socks. I tried to hide my disappointment, but I'm sure it was quite apparent. I cheered up when my mom said she had forgotten a gift in the hall outside the front room. I opened the door to the hall and magic happened. There stood a brand new, apple red Schwinn bike with a basket on the handle bars. It seemed to sparkle, like a diamond might to a newly engaged young lady.

The bike was not only a great surprise but also evidence of my mother's money management ability and devotion to her only child. Starting in the end of 1945, she had put away a dollar a week for 50 weeks to afford that bike.

What needs my mother did without to save a dollar a week I don't know, but it was the hallmark of her self-sacrifice. That self-denial was demonstrated even more clearly a few years earlier when she decided that her buck-toothed son needed braces. She would get a job and go without new silk stockings and new dresses for four years to accrue money for the Baltimore orthodontist, an astronomical sum at the time of $4,000. That bike meant many things to me—freedom to explore more of the countryside, equality with friends with bikes and a coveted job delivering our local paper, *The Evening Capital*.

The Evening Capital was located on Church Circle, on the opposite side of St. Anne's Church from the Reynold's Tavern library. The news room was located on the first floor and the press was sunk below the floor where the ground could hold its massive weight.

While the smell of printer's ink and the loud rolling of the press fascinated me, delivering papers wasn't as fun as I envisioned, nor as profitable. While we paper boys made a cent and a half on a five cent paper, we had to collect both our money and *The Evening Capital's*, often a difficult and sometimes impossible task (in an era when thirty cents could buy you a fine restaurant dinner or movie tickets for two.) Picking up and folding my papers at *The Capital*, I'd ride down College Avenue, with a stop at World War II naval housing in Bloomsbury Square next to St. John's College, ending at the Naval Academy wall on Hanover Street.

The need for braces showed up early, as can be seen in this photo of a buck-toothed, young Ralph Crosby. Four years of orthodontistry in Baltimore would straighten them later.

With papers delivered to historic mansions and decaying houses of poor families, my route led me to the grand houses connected to three of Maryland's four signers of the Declaration of Independence—Thomas Stone, Samuel Chase, and William Paca (pronounced "PAY-KAH") (Charles Carroll of Carrollton was the fourth). By their signatures on the Declaration, they put their homes, their fortunes and their lives on the line for an ideal and an idea, that the American colonies must gain freedom from British domination. Their stories of patriotism and heroism played out in their (and my) Annapolis hometown.

Thomas Stone and Peggy Stewart

When I delivered papers on Hanover Street, the house at 207, known as the Peggy Stewart House, was headquarters of the Anne Arundel County Board of Education. The board had tacked on a Victorian style porch and balcony to the front of the colonial mansion, which the next owner, J. Pierre Bernard, then President of Annapolis Bank and Trust, restored in the 1950s. In the 1970s, when I was elected to the bank's board, Pierre was its chairman and gave me the opportunity to explore the house from the inside when he entertained the board. In my day, the house faced the U.S. Naval Academy wall on Hanover Street with the back of the Chapel as its main view. In colonial times, before the Academy was built, it had a clear view of the Severn River.

While the house's historic significance includes ownership by signer Thomas Stone, it is even more significant as the home of Anthony Stewart, an Annapolis merchant who caused a firestorm when 17½ chests of tea from England were hidden in bales of cloth loaded on his brig Peggy Stewart, named for his daughter. Stewart paid the tax on the tea, a tax much opposed by patriots, so citizens wouldn't allow its unloading and demanded the ship be burned.

Fearing for his life, Stewart torched his ship himself and eventually left for Nova Scotia. Some historians feel the burning of the Peggy Stewart was a Revolutionary action of equal if not greater importance as the more famous Boston Tea Party of the previous year. In fact, one historian of the time wrote that it "far surpasses (The Boston Tea episode) in the apparent deliberation and utter carelessness of concealment, attending the bold measure which led to its accomplishment."

The Boston Tea Party stands out because England's parliament closed the Boston Harbor, while no such action was taken in Annapolis. And, as another writer concluded regarding the Stewart family:

The Peggy Stewart House, home to Annapolis merchant Anthony Stewart, who was forced to burn his own ship when he tried to smuggle English tea into Annapolis. (Collection of the Maryland State Archives)

In a final, fitting irony, their house on Hanover Street was sold in 1783 to Thomas Stone.

Even in Annapolis, Thomas Stone was the least known and least celebrated of the four signers, but he was no less a patriot. Stone was considered a talented lawyer and patriotic statesman by his contemporaries. They elected him to Congress in 1775, where he helped frame the Articles of Confederation. Stone was appointed President of Congress, pro tempore in 1784, while living at 207 Hanover Street. His residence there was only four years, cut short by his death at age 45.

Leaving Hanover Street, my paper route took me up Maryland Avenue to King George Street, across which on "Patriots' Walk" stood two of the greatest examples of colonial architecture. On the east corner stood the Hammond Harwood house, completed in 1776 and described as one of the finest classical dwellings in America. A national Historic Landmark, it was the town residence of Matthias Hammond, a wealthy planter and legislator. Its carved front entrance is considered one of the most beautiful doorways in America.

Ironically, the Peggy Stewart House was bought by lawyer and patriotic statesman Thomas Stone, one of Maryland's signers of the Declaration of Independence. (Collection of the Maryland Archives)

Samuel Chase

On the west corner, on property running a half a block up toward the State House, stood the Chase-Lloyd House, with its remarkable history. The Chase of "Chase-Lloyd" was Samuel Chase, called the "torch that lit the Revolutionary flame in Maryland." Torch-like he was, with a hot temper and an incendiary political oratory. He made radical speeches against the King of Great Britain long before his contemporaries.

Chase's strong stance against "taxation without representation," as embodied in the infamous Stamp Act, led him to organize the local Sons of Liberty with his friend William Paca. His fight for absolute independence while a member of Congress helped spur the Declaration of Independence, which he happily signed. A self-trained lawyer, Chase started out defending debtors since his lack of social status failed to attract wealthy clients. However, his prodigious legal skills and political ambitions opened many doors, ultimately including a door to the U.S. Supreme Court, nominated by his fellow patriot George Washington.

Chase made great friends (George Washington, William Paca) and powerful enemies (Thomas Jefferson). His opposition to Jefferson's policies led to his impeachment while a member of the U.S. Supreme Court. He was acquitted, which helped establish the precedent that judges should not be removed for political reasons. Chase served on the Supreme Court until his death in 1811.

Samuel Chase, called the "torch that lit the Revolutionary flame in Maryland," was a firebrand patriot who fought for absolute independence from Great Britain and gladly signed the Declaration of Independence. (Collection of the Maryland State Archives)

Seeing himself as arrived among the Maryland gentry in the years before the Revolution, Chase, desiring to build a brick mansion like his friend William Paca was building on nearby Prince George Street, purchased the corner lot at Maryland Avenue (then Northwest Street). When the cost of construction outstripped his finances, Chase sold the half-built home to Edward Lloyd IV, a wealthy plantation owner, and thus it became known as the Chase-Lloyd House. (An historical digression: Edward Lloyd IV's youngest daughter, Mary Tayloe Lloyd, was married to a young lawyer in the Chase-Lloyd house in 1802. His name was Francis Scott Key.)

Seeking to build a mansion like some of his wealthy Annapolis contemporaries, Samuel Chase ran out of money and sold his Maryland Avenue property to wealthy planter Edward Lloyd IV, giving the house the double name, the Chase-Lloyd House. (Collection of the Maryland State Archives)

Through a series of marriages and sales, a descendant of Samuel Chase, Hester Ann Chase Ridout, inherited the Chase-Lloyd house and, in her will, established it as a residence for elderly women "where they may find retreat from the vicissitudes of life," which it remains today.

William Paca and Carvel Hall

Delivering papers to homes on King George Street took me past the tree-lined, horseshoe driveway entrance to Annapolis' grand hotel, Carvel Hall. Elegant in its own right, Carvel Hall had added allure because it was connected to, and built on the one-time garden of, William Paca's mansion.

Carvel Hall, Annapolis' grand hotel, site of many of my youthful escapades, was built on the garden of and encompassed the manor house of patriot William Paca. His home, shown here, was used as the hotel's reception area. (Collection of the Maryland State Archives)

Using his wife Mary's wealth, four days after their wedding in 1763, William Paca purchased a double lot, back to back, one facing Prince George Street, the other fronting King George, to build his thirty-seven room home. The house served as a dwelling until 1907, when it was purchased for construction of a 200-room hotel on the two-acre garden site facing King George Street. The hotel used the Paca House as a reception and registration center.

The hotel was named Carvel Hall in honor of an enormously popular 1899 book, *Richard Carvel*, written by the American Winston Churchill, a distant relation of the famed British Prime Minister and noted author of the same name. To avoid confusion, the latter agreed to sign his books, "Winston Spencer Churchill."

Carvel Hall became a social center of Annapolis and was the preferred lodging of legislators and visitors to the Naval Academy. Carvel Hall was an oft visited spot for me. I would enter the Paca House doorway, differentiated from William Paca's time only by the sign, "Carvel Hall" over the portico entrance. I would go there to meet friends whose grandmother lived there, or sit in William Paca's front parlor with my late date, or to ogle my peers dancing in the hotel ballroom at cotillion. I mocked them, but I was jealous. My parents had neither the inclination nor the money to send me to learn to dance. I learned the informal way, in the houses of girl friends who taught me to jitterbug, then slow dance to rhythm and blues music or the likes of Nat King Cole. Carvel Hall has a special place in my heart because my first date with my wife-to-be, Carlotta, was a dance party there on January 1, 1955. I was 21; she was 17.

That blind date came about because on New Year's morning I visited my college roommate, Fred Wiedenbauer, at his family's upstairs apartment on Shipwright Street, across from the historic home of Upton Scott, the uncle of Francis Scott Key. Key spent his grammar school through college years at St. Johns living with Upton Scott's family.

That 1955 morning, Fred invited me to a party a local guys' group was having at Carvel Hall. Dateless, I called Fred's date for the evening, Margaret, a girl I had previously dated, to see if any of her friends was available for me to take to the party. She informed me that an attractive young lady had recently arrived from San Diego, California, and would see if she was interested.

Margaret called back to say this California girl might go to the party but wanted to talk to me first. A long telephone conversation with Carlotta ensued, and a date was agreed to.

Fred and Margaret drove me to Carlotta's house that evening, and when I entered I met a beautiful, raven-haired young lady with a slight overbite that reminded me of the lovely actress Ann Blythe. Carlotta's combined Mexican and Scottish heritage produced a lovely olive skin and hair so dark that in grammar school she was called "Black Beauty." I was smitten on the spot. That night at Carvel Hall we danced to the Drifters' version of White Christmas and talked about our next date. Did we click? Suffice to say that, at this writing, Carlotta and I have been married for 57 years. As fate would have it, Fred's apartment was even crucial in my courting of Carlotta. After college, Fred moved out of his apartment and, after studying at the local hospital to be an x-ray technician, Carlotta and a girlfriend moved in. That's where she lived when I proposed.

Guests entering Carvel Hall were usually greeted by Marcellus Hall, an Annapolis legend, the hotel's bell captain, one of the most pleasant and respected black men in town. Hall treated us interloping youngsters wandering the hotel halls with a great deal of forbearance and his perennial smile. He winked at us late-daters, as long as we behaved. Marcellus worked at Carvel Hall from 1913 until it closed its doors in 1965. Then, the hotel was torn down and the Paca House threatened with demolition until the preservation group, Historic Annapolis, Inc., took it over and restored both the house and garden.

William Paca, a Maryland signer of the Declaration of Independence, whose patriotic fervor led George Washington to declare: "If it weren't for William Paca, and others like him, there would be no United States of America." (Collection of the Maryland State Archives)

William Paca lived in the house only until 1774, when his wife Mary died. While her death ended his affection for the house, William Paca's affection for liberty was stronger than ever. Not only had he partnered with Samuel Chase in organizing the Sons of Liberty opposition to the Stamp Act, he became a Maryland delegate to the First Continental Congress and, of course, a willing signer of the Declaration of Independence. During the Revolution, Paca spent thousands of dollars of his own money to supply American troops. After the war, in 1782, Paca was elected to three successive terms as governor of Maryland, and among his first ceremonial duties were to welcome Congress to the temporary capital of the new country. In 1787, Paca championed amendments to the new Constitution to protect the rights of citizens, including freedom of speech, freedom of the press and the right to trial by jury, harbingers of the Bill of Rights, finally ratified by the states in 1791. Paca's patriotic fervor led George Washington to declare: "If it weren't for William Paca, and others like him, there would be no United States of America." One man "like him" was Charles Carroll of Carrollton.

Charles Carroll of Carrollton

While the home of Charles Carroll of Carrollton wasn't on my paper route, it was even more infused in my life—and the life of Annapolis—than the other signers' homes. Charles Carroll of Carrollton was born in the home started by his grandfather, Charles Carroll the Settler, and expanded by his father, Charles Carroll of Annapolis. The Carrolls, of Irish Catholic ancestry, came to Maryland under the patronage of Lord Baltimore, and in 1701 the Settler purchased a large tract of land on Spa Creek (at one time called "Carroll's Creek") at the foot of Duke of Gloucester Street running all the way to Church (Main) Street. The Settler became the largest landholder in Maryland, and his son and grandson were among the wealthiest men in America.

Despite their wealth, the Carrolls, as Catholics, were treated as second-class citizens, without the right to vote, to operate their own schools and churches or to practice law. Into that world in 1737 was born the third generation Carroll, so ill as a child, he didn't seem destined for a long, productive life. How wrong that was! Suffice it to say, he rode his horse 10 miles a day at age 93.

Since Catholics could have no church in Annapolis, Charles Carroll of Carrollton provided them a chapel in his mansion. It wasn't until after the Revolution that religious freedom allowed

Catholics in Maryland to build their own churches, and the first one in Annapolis, St. Mary's, was built in 1823 at Charles Carroll of Carrollton's direction on property he donated up the street from his home. Thirty years later, Carroll's granddaughters sold the entire Carroll property to the Redemptorist fathers, including the original St. Mary's Church property and the Carroll mansion. The Redemptorists built a new church and, eventually, on some of Carroll's Duke of Gloucester Street lots, a grammar school and, much later, a high school were built.

Among the wealthiest men in America, Charles Carroll of Carrollton put everything on the line to support the revolution. A catholic, who had suffered from protestant religious discrimination, he became the only person of his religion to sign the Declaration of Independence. (Collection of the Maryland State Archives)

Though I'm not Catholic, St. Mary's had an ongoing impact on my life. Three blocks from our 183 Main Street apartment, St. Mary's dominates the landscape with its cross-topped spire, an Annapolis landmark and navigating point for mariners rising above surrounding structures, joining its fellow towers standing guard over the city—the State House, St. Anne's Church and the Naval Academy Chapel. Built in 1853, this church sat on an acre of beautiful property in my youth, flanked on one side by the Carroll mansion on Spa Creek and its parochial schools on the other.

The then playing field behind the church and grammar school was another of my playgrounds. In fact, on that field I learned to play lacrosse, the quintessential Maryland sport that I passed on to my son and grandchildren, which we played in high school and college.

In later years, St. Mary's was to mean a whole lot more to me. Since my wife was Catholic, my three children were baptized there. I watched them grow as St. Mary's students, and I walked my youngest daughter, Belinda, down the church aisle at her wedding and watched my son, Ray, get married there—not to mention the academic, sporting and social events I've attended at St. Mary's as father and grandfather. There's something wonderful about the family continuity of church and school in a small town, especially watching two generations of youngsters growing up.

Scene of many of my boyhood adventures, Charles Carroll of Carrollton's Spa Creekside property, part of which he devoted for construction of St. Mary's Church, shown here next to Carroll's mansion. The entire property eventually was sold to the Redemptorist order of priests. (Collection of the Maryland State Archives)

The St. Mary's playing field led to a grassy hill, past the mansion, to a long seawall lined with beautiful, old weeping willows standing like sentinels for the passing boats. The pier there afforded me a fine fishing and crabbing spot. Friends and I played hide and seek among the ancient privet hedges, planted in the 1700s, that grew between the old house and the water. I'd also gaze at the old, discolored tomb stones of departed priests in the burial plot beyond the house.

I must admit that back then I gave little thought to the home that hosted George Washington and the Marquis de Lafayette, among other revolutionary leaders, and housed one of our greatest patriots. It was only as an adult that I would enter the house and explore those historic rooms where Charles Carroll of Carrollton helped change history. Carroll began his overt opposition to British rule in 1772 when he wrote his essays for the *Maryland Gazette* opposing taxation without representation. His letters debated Daniel Dulaney, who represented the proprietary establishment.

Daniel Dulaney was scion of the wealthy Dulaney family, whose patriarch, Daniel Sr., rose from indentured servant from Ireland to successful lawyer and landed gentry in the space of ten years. The Senior Dulaney went from defender of Marylanders' rights to leading defender of proprietary interests and became the beneficiary of Lord Baltimore's patronage, assuming several executive offices in the colony. He passed on his wealth, influence and politics to his eldest son Daniel. The Dulaneys and the Carrolls had feuded for years over common-owned businesses and that feud heated up as the Revolution approached. When the younger Daniel Dulaney began a letter-wiring campaign in the Maryland Gazette to support his British loyalist position, using the pseudonym "Antilon," Charles Carroll of Carrolton replied anonymously as "First Citizen," and over six months of Gazette discourse, Carroll won over the public's favor. Once his authorship as "First Citizen" was made public, Carroll drew the accolades of Maryland patriots, who looked to him for leadership. He was even crucial in the decision to burn the Peggy Stewart.

In the Peggy Stewart incident in 1773, Anthony Stewart appealed to Charles Carroll to intervene in his behalf with the angry mob, but Carroll told Stewart the only answer was to burn the cargo and the ship. Around that time a group led by Carroll, called the "Popular Party," actively opposed the proprietary government. The group included Carroll's relative (and my hierarchical neighbor) Charles Carroll the Barrister, Samuel Chase and William Paca.

In 1775 Carroll of Carrollton went with a Popular Party delegation to the Second Continental Congress, where he was elected to the Council of Safety. Thus, by winning election, he overcame the prevailing anti-Catholic rules and personified religious toleration, which would become a result of the Revolution and a hallmark of our constitution. On August 2, 1776, Carroll became the only Catholic to sign the Declaration of Independence, risking all in the cause of the colonies.

In fact, more than 50 years after signing the Declaration, Carroll then told famous French writer on American politics, Alexis de Tocqueville, that he had risked, together with his life, the "most considerable fortune there was in America."

Carroll's leadership was recognized after the war when, in 1789, he became one of Maryland's first two U.S. Senators, and in 1792 he was even proposed as a candidate for President of the United States. In 1826, Charles Carroll became the last surviving signer of the Declaration with the deaths of Thomas Jefferson and John Adams, ironically on the same fateful day, July 4. Carroll passed away in 1832, his 96th year, and was honored by a national day of mourning. *The Baltimore American*, a paper I would one day work for, carried the headline: "Charles Carroll of Carrollton is no more. The last of the signers is dead!" U.S. President Andrew Jackson closed government offices in Washington, D.C., and the *Maryland Gazette* reported that Maryland's Governor George Howard ordered a day of mourning for Carroll, including "thirteen minute guns be fired, at sunrise, at noon and at sunset." In a book of biographical sketches of the signers, written in 1848, author B.J. Lossing said of Carroll, "When Jefferson and Adams died, he was the last vestige that remained upon earth of that holy brotherhood, who stood sponsor at the baptism in blood of our infant Republic."

Visiting the Carroll House now, as I did on a lovely spring day researching this book, takes me back to my childhood and into the colonial past. The quiet greenery of the Carroll House gardens stands in almost silent observation of water-born and waterborne Annapolis as it has for more than 300 years.

In my adult years, I've visited the Carroll House numerous times for meetings and parties in the garden and inside the house. The four-story, Georgian brick mansion appears as sturdy today as when it was built in the mid-1700s. The Redemptorist cemetery with grave stones dating back to the 1800s still overlooks what was Carroll's Creek, today's Spa Creek.

At the top of the hill, at the front entrance to the house, the landscape has also changed from colonial days and the days of my youth. A parking lot has replaced the ball field I played on, which undoubtedly had been a greenscape in Charles Carroll's day.

I was reminded of Carroll's time when I stumbled up on the remains of a rustic red stone wall on the water side of the house. A plaque commemorating the wall reads: "In 1770, work began with the construction of a stone wall of 'Severn Stone' and would not be completed until 1775."

I was reminded of my youth looking out on Spa Creek, despite the modern condominiums lining the Eastport shore, by the sailboat circling leisurely on the Creek waiting for the bridge to open so it could sail into the Severn and by the young man at the oars of a row boat heading up the Creek. I couldn't tell if he had a crab net aboard, but I bet he did.

CHAPTER NINE

A PASSION FOR PRINTER'S INK

If you went two doors up from our apartment at 183 Main and took the short cut through the movie lot and the gate behind the Pappas house and out onto Duke of Gloucester Street, you'd end up at the head of Charles Street. Two long downhill blocks, ending at Spa Creek, Charles Street played a crucial role in Annapolis history, the country's history and my history.

One of the four signers' good friends and revolutionary supporter lived at 124 Charles Street, as did one of my childhood friends. Their friend was Jonas Green, publisher of the *Maryland Gazette*. My friend was Scott Bowers, an eighth generation descendant of Jonas Green.

The Jonas Green House, where I played with a boyhood friend, is where Green, *Maryland Gazette* publisher, met with his friend, Benjamin Franklin. Jonas Green, Maryland's official printer in the mid-1700s, stoked the revolution with his newspaper's opposition to the hated British Stamp Act. He and his family, printers all, helped turn public opinion against onerous British laws. (Collection of the Maryland State Archives)

In the rooms of the Jonas Green House, with its early 1700s' broad wood floors, its wide colonial fireplace for cooking, and its narrow stairs to the second floor, Scott and I, in our grammar school days, often played and ate snacks after romping on Charles Street. In those same rooms, Jonas Green ate and chatted with his friend and mentor, Benjamin Franklin.

Green had apprenticed in Franklin's print shop in Philadelphia, and when Franklin heard that Maryland needed a public printer, he steered his friend to Annapolis, whence Green moved with his wife, Anne Catherine, to 124 Charles Street. Green came from a family of printers. His grandfather, Samuel Green, had been the public printer for Massachusetts. Having taken over as Maryland's official printer, Green followed Franklin's lead and started a newspaper, taking the name of the State's since abandoned first newspaper the *Maryland Gazette*, printing it in a small shed behind the house.

The predecessor *Maryland Gazette* was founded by William Parks in 1727. Parks, a publisher in England, came to the colony based on promises of printing work by Maryland legislators. He brought presses across the ocean with him in 1725 and went to work in Annapolis as Public Printer for Maryland, later starting the *Maryland Gazette* as a sideline. The offer of a lucrative salary from the Virginia legislature lured Parks away from Maryland, and the *Gazette* ceased printing until Jonas Green arrived on the scene in 1738. In an historic sidelight, in 1730, when Parks went on a trip to England, he left management of his Annapolis paper and print shop to an employee by the name of John Peter Zenger.

Power of the Press

That name became very familiar to me as a journalism student in college. In the journalism text books, Zenger's name was synonymous with freedom of the press. An indentured printer's apprentice following his emigration from Germany, Zenger ultimately operated his own print shop in Chestertown, on Maryland's Eastern Shore, before joining Parks as printer and editor. Zenger later moved to New York in 1733 and founded his own paper. Arrested for publishing criticism (called "seditious libel") of the royalist governor of New York, he spent eight months in jail before being acquitted by a jury in a surprise verdict, one which contradicted British rulings that harsh attacks on government were seditious even if true. This ruling was an important step in the journey to the First Amendment to our Constitution. In a separate but complementary action, in 1777, Maryland became the first state to grant freedom of the press.

Newspapers played a key role in fomenting the American Revolution, being the only means of widespread communication. As explained by Norman K. Risjord, in his book *Builders of Annapolis*:

> *Although the papers were small, consisting usually of four pages on a single folded sheet of paper, poorly printed, and relatively expensive, their weekly appearance was eagerly awaited. The news in them might be from three to eight weeks old, due to the slowness of the post and dissemination by travelers, but it was fresh to its readers. There was as yet no concept of an editorial, but contributions from readers, usually protected by pseudonyms, carried forth the public debate. Each edition was small in numbers, due to the primitive condition of the printer's art, but the sheets were eagerly passed from hand to hand, nailed to the walls of taverns, and sent in batches to relatives in the countryside. Newspapers were crucial to the creation of the American Republic.*
>
> *Among the most important of the journalistic torchbearers of the Revolution were Jonas and Catherine Green. Their vehicle was the* Maryland Gazette *of Annapolis.*

One such anonymous contribution in the *Maryland Gazette*, mentioned earlier, was between "Antilon" (Daniel Dulaney), writing from the proprietary government's point of view, opposed by "First Citizen" (Charles Carroll of Carrollton), writing in opposition to the proprietary, a verbal battle in which Carroll won the public's favor.

Green's *Maryland Gazette* turned public opinion even more against British lawmaking over The Stamp Act of 1765, which levied a prohibitive tax on use of paper, including newspapers and pamphlets. While colonists generally disliked the tax, Green opposed it on two levels, patriotically and financially. His first reaction was to publish the papers with a skull and crossbones printed where the stamp was supposed to be affixed. He fully intended to stop publishing, but was persuaded to continue the battle against tyranny. Green's following issues of the paper carried headlines satirizing its impending death at the hands of British Parliament. The first was headed, "*Maryland Gazette*

Expiring: In uncertain Hopes of a Resurrection to Life again." For the next three weeks the paper was called a "Supplement" to the "last regular issue of October 10th." Then, after a month's silence, there appeared "The Apparition of the *Maryland Gazette*. Which is Not Dead But Sleepeth." On January 20, 1766, came an issue headed "*The Maryland Gazette* Reviving," followed on February 20 by an issue titled "*The Maryland Gazette* Revived."

Jonas Green displayed his opposition to the Stamp Act by publishing the
Maryland Gazette with a skull and crossbones where the onerous stamp was
supposed to be affixed. (Collection of the Maryland State Archives)

In March, the Stamp Act was repealed, and the plain *"Maryland Gazette"* appeared, but the dye was cast. The *Maryland Gazette* and similar colonial newspapers carried the revolutionary words of such patriots as Patrick Henry, supporting the rising anti-crown sentiment in the colonies.

The Stamp Act repeal was Jonas Green's last crusade. He died in early April 1767, and Anne Catherine Green carried on his work, both as Maryland's public printer and publisher of the *Gazette*, and she carried on the editorial fight for freedom. She died before the Revolution, but her son Frederick, later aided by his brother Samuel, continued to be a leading supporter of the Revolution. The paper stayed in the family until 1839.

Charles Street Revisited

Speaking of the Green family, while retracing my youthful footsteps on Charles Street in preparation for this book, I happened upon a gentleman cleaning the front stoop at number 124. He turned out to be Scott Bowers' cousin, Randall Brown, also an eighth generation descendant of Jonas Green. Randy now lived in the family home and invited me in. In the living room, which I vaguely remembered from bygone years, Randy recounted others who had met there, including Benjamin Franklin and the Tuesday Club. The Tuesday Club was a colonial Annapolis institution that met on Tuesdays, usually in members' homes, for conversation and comedy. The members and their guests were mostly successful merchants, politicians and lawyers, but tradesmen such as Jonas Green also were elected to membership, thus blurring the lines of social class, presaging the American democracy as opposed to British aristocracy. Randy also noted how Benjamin Franklin's relationship with Jonas Green was marred by debts. Franklin supplied Green with paper from Philadelphia on promises to pay, which Green failed to keep current, thus damaging their relationship. According to Randy Brown, after Jonas Green's death, his wife Anne Catherine paid off the debt to Franklin.

My brush with newspaper history in the Green house was but one of many experiences that whetted my appetite for journalism. Around age 10, my friend John Henneberger and I made a childish attempt to develop a comic book. John, who lived directly across from our Green Street grammar school, was a willing partner in many childhood escapades—from exploring the city dock to exploring his father's restaurant, the Mirror Grill, at the v-shaped corner of Main and Francis Streets.

My newspaper experience went from watching the presses print the local papers I was to deliver to selling papers on Main Street on Saturday nights. On Saturday evenings in Annapolis, residents, farmers and watermen would converge on Main Street, and several of us youngsters would sell them the Saturday night edition of the Sunday papers, *The Baltimore Sun* and, my favorite, Hearst's *Baltimore News-American*. The latter undoubtedly appealed to me because, unlike the staid old *Sun*, the outer section of the *News-American* was the colorful comics, not the front page.

After selling papers on Saturday night, I'd take home a *News-American* and spread it out on my bed. I'd read the full-color comic pages first; my favorite strips were *Prince Valiant* and *The Katzenjammer Kids*. Next would come the sports pages. Once in a while, some news or feature item would catch my eye, and I'd be fascinated by the story telling. Hindsight tells me those Saturday nights, the comic book caper, reporting for my high school paper and Jonas Green's house, helped fashion my career as a journalist, which began after college when I joined the News-American Company.

One of the pals I sold papers with on Saturday nights was long-time friend Tommy Steward. Tommy also lived on Charles Street, across from the Jonas Green House. Tommy's family apartment appeared no different than most middle-class apartments of the day, but it was one half of what once had been a grand colonial home known as the Adams-Kilty House, built in the late 1770s by William Adams, a delegate to the colonial General Assembly. It was purchased by William Kilty in 1799; thus the dual title. Historic though it was, we paid that little heed, nailing a basketball backboard and net to its ancient brick side and generally abusing the structure with balls of all sorts.

Tommy and I would often gather friends for sports at the bottom of Charles Street, where there was a vacant lot perfect for football and baseball games. We played outdoors almost all the time. With little in-the-home entertainment in the days before television, we entertained ourselves.

Sandlot football was our favorite game, and "sand lot" was an appropriate name. We'd play football wherever we found half-a-dozen or more guys to play. For example, we played on the movie lot, next door to the Republic Theater, undeterred by the cinders and stones in knees when you were knocked down. The hard-packed dirt of the Charles Street field was not much more forgiving.

The vacant lot on Charles Street looked out on Acton's Cove, an inlet off of Spa Creek that had great historic significance. When settlers of Providence looked for farming land, Richard Acton claimed a 100-acre parcel on the south side of the Severn River between two creeks that would eventually be known as Spa Creek and College Creek. Thus, Richard Acton would be among the first residents of what would become Annapolis.

On the other side of the vacant lot/ball field was the Annapolis Emergency Hospital, where I was born and my children would be born. While the hospital bill for delivering our children in the 1960s was about $300 each, it cost my parents $48.10 for me for a 10-day stay. My mother was discharged with me on Christmas day 1933, and the bill reads:

> *For 10 Days Board.........................30.00*
> *For Use of Operating Room...........10.00*
> *For Special Prescriptions....................60*
> *For Laboratory Fee...........................2.50*
> *Nursery Charges..............................5.00*
>   48.10

The bill for my mother's stay in the Annapolis Emergency Hospital for my birth in 1933 was $48.10—for a 10 days stay!

When in the 1990s the hospital finally moved from that spot, which it had occupied in one form or another for almost 100 years, condominiums and houses were built in its place by a company that became a client of my marketing agency. So, having the duty to name the development, I called it "Acton's Landing." When Lord Baltimore established Maryland ports of entry where goods could only be loaded and unloaded, one of the places named was "att (sic) Richard Acton's land in Arundell County."

When we could assemble only four or five players for a football game, we'd wander up the hill to the softer, small green lawn in front of nearby Acton Hall, a great colonial home built by John Hammond in the early 1770s and named for Richard Acton. John was the brother of Mathias Hammond, builder of the Hammond-Harwood House, on Maryland Avenue, another of the finest classical, colonial dwellings in America. Thus at another hangout, I mingled with history. There were more to come.

CHAPTER TEN

OTHER HAVENS AND HANGOUTS

Acton's Cove, the library and the pool room were not the only havens and hangouts of my youth. Television had not come to lower-middle-class homes in the 1930s and 40s, and electronic devices were something we read about in Buck Rogers' stories and Dick Tracy comics. As teenagers we spent most of our leisure hours outside the home, and the main indoor hangout of my generation was the drug store with its lunch counter and/or mini-restaurant.

These gathering places featured soda fountains and juke boxes or wall boxes that allowed us to play songs for a nickel per play. Across Main Street from our apartment were two such drug store soda fountains, one in Read's drug store; the other in T. Kent Green's drug store. For a nickel Coke or a ten cent ice cream soda, we'd sit for hours listening to our favorite music while avoiding the waitresses' dirty looks.

Filling prescriptions seemed like a sideline of these drug stores, which sold everything from cigarettes to cosmetics, candy and condoms. The soda fountain lunch counter, with its spinning high stool seats, would serve up sandwiches, soups and ice cream concoctions, such as banana splits, to young and old alike. Among my favorites were the inexpensive flavored cokes—chocolate or cherry—mixed before your eyes out of syrups and seltzer water.

Equally popular were the ice cream parlors or luncheonettes, smaller restaurants also featuring counters. Several were within a stone's throw from 183 Main Street. Bernstein's, a family run ice cream parlor with light food, was on the first floor of the apartment house where my grandparents lived. (In later years, it became "Chick & Ruth's Delly" (sic), somewhat of an Annapolis institution.)

My favorite high school hangout, on Main Street across the street from Bernstein's was the Wardroom Restaurant, run by the Bounelis brothers, Angel and George. The main attractions of the Wardroom were the pinball machines that sat just inside the front door. I spent many a nickel there trying to beat the bouncing metal ball to produce a payoff in clinking nickels spewing from the machine. The clinking sounds were few and far between.

Further down Main Street was a tiny diner called "The New Grill," run by a young man, Johnny Cristo, known around town for his restaurant prowess and gambling nature. Even though I was a high school student, much younger than Johnny, we competed, but without gambling. We played chess in one of his diner's booths. At the time, I was president of the Annapolis High School chess club.

Johnny was one of the many Greeks who found success in running restaurants in Annapolis. The Bounelises who ran the Wardroom were joined up the street by Bounelis cousins who ran the Capitol Hotel and restaurant. On Maryland Avenue, my friend Angie Nichols' family owned the Little Campus restaurant, and Greeks ran the G&J Grill up the street from the Little Campus. G&J was a favorite gathering place for my high school crowd, drawn by its colorful orange faux leather booths with Formica tables and patient soda jerks. On West Street, just around the corner from Church Circle was the Royal Restaurant, run by the Pantelides family.

The West Street Little Tavern, where I sometimes grabbed a burger breakfast, when the tiny hamburgers cost only a nickel. (Collection of the Maryland State Archives)

But Main Street was restaurant central. The father of my classmate, John Alvanos, affectionately known as "Greek," ran John's Tavern in the middle of Main Street, and nearby was the city's second Little Tavern. Those ten cent hamburgers are forever tasted In the memory of my youthful peers; tiny burgers fried on a greasy grill with onions sautéed alongside of them, then popped on a tiny bun and topped with ketchup, mustard or both. I know I'm not the only one with that memory because someone invariably mentions it at a class reunion.

But the restaurant food most etched in my memory was La Rosa's pizza, a subtle mix of cheese and Mama Maggio's sauce on homemade dough, a mouthwatering combination the equal of which I have never found. La Rosa's was a Main Street institution run by Harry and Joe Maggio, two enormously likeable Italian brothers, who turned their father Sam's hotel and bowling alley into our go to eatery. La Rosa's was a place for end-of-date rendezvous or an end of weekend snack with buddies. I took my future wife there on our second date.

My special appreciation for restaurants goes back to my early childhood. For our family, a meal at a restaurant was a special occasion. Our eatery of choice was Mandris Confectionary, located on the corner of Market Space and Randall Street, diagonal from the City Dock and two blocks from the Naval Academy's Gate Number One. While we seldom ate out when I was a youngster, every month or two we would head for Mandris' on a weekend with a dollar and change in Mom's purse. Why the dollar and change? Because it would feed all three of us.

Mom and I would order a roast beef dinner with mashed potatoes, gravy and a green vegetable, and dad would order fresh ham (uncured pork) with similar side dishes. Bread and butter were included. Mom and Dad would get coffee, and I would have a soft drink. The meals were 30 cents each; the drinks five cents. Total cost $1.05 plus a ten cent tip. While one dollar in the early 1940s would be worth about $15 in the 90s, that three-person meal would cost at least $45 today, which is probably more than what my father's weekly salary was back then.

While Annapolis' restaurant food was a treat for me, like most of us, nothing was better than mom's home cooking. She produced some wonderful meals in the little kitchen at 183 Main Street. The most luxurious, of course, was Thanksgiving dinner with its traditional turkey, sausage stuffing, mashed potatoes and gravy, cranberry sauce, sauerkraut and homemade biscuits and butter.

There would be pumpkin or apple pie for dessert, but my unique dessert was another biscuit covered in gravy. Thanksgiving aside, if I had to choose favorite meals prepared by my mother; here's my list:

Breakfast: Dough ditties and salt mackerel. The deep fried dough smothered in butter accompanied by the salty taste of the fish (soaked in water overnight to reduce some of the overpowering salinity) was a Sunday special.

Lunch: A plain old baloney and American cheese sandwich with lettuce and yellow mustard. I liked it so much, mom would pack one for my lunch almost every day of my high school years.

Dinner: It's a tossup between 1. pork chops and spaghetti, with the chops simmered in the tomato sauce, giving it a unique sweetness and 2. fried chicken with peas and dumplings, with emphasis on the peas and dumplings, overcooked to produce their own pasty but tasty sauce.

Dessert: Mom's homemade raisin tarts, creamy raisins in a round, dough boat with a cross of pastry on top.

Mandris Confectionary, one of my childhood favorite restaurants, was a successor to Middleton's Tavern, a colonial eatery that fed the likes of Washington, Jefferson and Franklin. Mandris' was later modernized and rechristened Middleton's Tavern. (Collection of the Maryland State Archives)

For me, no meal at Mandris' could compare with that menu.

Mandris' took its name from the family that originally owned it. The original owners' daughter, Mary Mandris, married Cleo Apostol, and they operated it for thirty-five years, including the time we ate there. Their son John, who followed me to Annapolis High, became Mayor of Annapolis. Mandris' was also a great stop going to and from the Academy because it also held a case full of penny candy.

At Mandris', too, we touched American history, eating where the likes of Washington, Jefferson and Franklin ate. In the mid-1700s, Horatio Middleton, owner of a ferry that linked Annapolis to the Eastern Shore, built a building on this site and advertised it as an "Inn For Sea-Faring Men." Not only was "Middleton Tavern," as it came to be known, used as a meeting place for the famous Tuesday Club and its guest Ben Franklin, it was frequented by members of the Continental Congress at times such as Washington's resignation and ratification of the Treaty of Paris.

Middleton Tavern was an important stopping place for early travelers catching Middleton's ferry across the Chesapeake Bay. Tench Tilghman, on his way to Philadelphia with the message of Cornwallis' surrender, stopped at the tavern, as did Thomas Jefferson, whose records state that in 1783 he paid Horatio's son, Samuel Middleton, for ferry passage to the Eastern Shore. In 1968, a distant relative of mine, Jerry Hardesty, bought Mandris restaurant from the Apostols, renovated it, and changed the name back to Middleton Tavern, under which it continues today.

Across the street from Mandris' was the City Market House, which had been the center of Annapolis' food trade in its head-of-the-City-Dock location since 1784. When I was twelve or thirteen, half the Market House was empty, and a gym opened in that empty half facing Mandris'. At first called the "Metropolitan Athletic Club" when it opened in 1945, it featured weight lifting, punching bags and wrestling mats, and had as many as 100 boys as members. When I joined for a short period, my friends and I came under the tutelage of Reggie Faust, Annapolis' answer to strong man Charles Atlas, America's muscled guru of the era. By the time the gym became Annapolis Strength and Health Club in 1949, I had quit. I should have continued; I could have used more muscle.

While the club had that sweaty gym smell, it was mixed with the strong odor of seafood. In the other half of the building a market continued, including several seafood shops, a meat market, a deli and a fruit and vegetable stand. The gym closed in 1950, when the City decided to rent the space to more shops. The City Market House, actually the eighth iteration somewhere in downtown Annapolis, remained in my youth and remains now remarkably similar in appearance to when it was built in the center of Market Square at the head of the City Dock in 1858. It has survived several suggestions it be demolished and has been renovated repeatedly. But it survives, and I have fond memories of eating giant sandwiches from John Schley's delicatessen and purchasing hand-cut steaks from Mac's Meat market. Almost everything you ever wanted to know about the City Market is available in Annapolis writer Ginger Doyel's book, *Gone to MARKET: The Annapolis Market House, 1698-2005.*

About the time I quit going to the gym another hangout opened. The City briefly ran a teen center on Conduit Street, to help keep us teens out of trouble, though I don't recall many kids getting in trouble. If you left the alley leading from my "back yard" at the time, the building on the right housed side-by-side 1870s store fronts with big glass windows meant to admit more light to the stores' interiors to better display the merchandise inside. The display in the first store, at 171 Conduit Street, was unintentional—a bevy of pinball machines in E.J. Kramer's slot machine business. That's the store whose back wall I used as a ball bounce-back practicing my tennis and lacrosse.

The next store, 169 Conduit, housed the Teen Center, where we jitterbugged to records and drank copious cokes. I remember 169 much more for the shop that preceded the Teen Center, Eddie Leonard's Sporting Goods store. When I was around twelve, my parents shattered their budget to buy me a first baseman's claw mitt at Eddie Leonard's. Without the fingers of the normal baseball glove, the claw mitt is more like a catcher's mitt, though not as padded. Longer than the normal glove with a wider, deeper pocket, it allowed the first baseman to scoop up errant throws more easily. Since first base had become my position in our pick up softball games, the claw mitt was a godsend in my error-prone youth. As in many youthful experiences, the claw mitt supplied a tough lesson.

After playing softball one day at St. John's, I foolishly left my glove outside the nearby gymnasium when I went in to play on the gymnastic equipment. When I returned, the glove was gone. I lost my red, Schwinn bike the same way, leaving it unguarded in the Republic Theater's parking lot while I watched a film. It's a shame that treasured play things my parents scrimped for to buy me, I was so neglectful to protect. However, lesson learned the hard way.

While I enjoyed hanging out at these havens with my contemporaries, I hardly ever partook of the fads of the forties and fifties. I never owned a hula hoop, and when I tried a friend's I had a hard time getting that colorful, circular plastic tube to rotate around my body. I never owned a pair of saddle shoes, though these shoes with the mostly black saddle-shaped decorative panel placed mid foot, were all the rage, especially among the girls, who paired them with white "bobby sox." I did get a Slinky as a present one Christmas, and I loved seeing it walk by itself down the long staircase leading from our apartment. What I enjoyed most as a teenager was sports, and living in Annapolis I had the most unique playgrounds to practice all sorts of athletics.

Chapter Eleven

A Unique Playground

St. John's College

As I have said, in my youth Annapolis was such a small town, you could walk just about anywhere you wanted to go. For me it was an easy one block trip from State House hill to a campus of sports venues and quiet history—St. John's College.

It's a bit strange that St. John's, known for its "Great Books" curriculum, where students study everything from Aristotle to Newton, and a college that forsook intercollegiate athletics in the 1930s, would be the major athletic arena of my youth. Not that St. John's was never a haven for athletes. Back in the 1920s and early 30s the college won national championships in lacrosse. In fact, one of my uncles by marriage played intercollegiate football at St. John's when it was a military academy.

For me, the vestiges of the college's early sports incarnation provided a proper diamond for pick up softball, clay courts where I learned to play tennis, basketball in an ancient gymnasium and "sandlot" football on a wonderful grassy field overlooking College Creek, the northern boundary of St. John's and, back then, also of Annapolis. The creek meandered next door through the U.S. Naval Academy on its way to the Severn River.

The two colleges were separated by King George Street, and the bridge over the creek provided me with a fishing platform beneath its Annapolis side and a way to sneak into Navy baseball games beneath what was then the West Annapolis side. The platform, jutting out into the Creek like a square little pier, but hidden from view, made me feel as if I had found my own cave. Except for the sound of cars rumbling over the bridge above, I was in a world apart. Fishing on the platform, probably a repair space for utilities that ran under the bridge, was a refuge from the outside world, and as an only child I had no trouble being alone, weaving my own adventure. But fish I did, usually catching a few perch. I recall my most memorable catch there, an eel about three feet long, so slippery and wriggling, I couldn't get my hook out of its mouth. I'm sure I felt I was fighting a dragon. After struggling five or more minutes with the eel, it won. I threw it back in the creek along with my hook, line and sinker.

Sneaking into Navy baseball games from under the bridge was a regular occurrence in spring. I'm sure the ticket sellers closed their eyes to my transgressions—especially since a couple of them were my uncles by marriage. (I often got similar treatment at Navy Basketball games in Dahlgren Hall.) The extra fun of Navy baseball games was taking care of the scoreboard in left field by posting the score, hanging black, wooden plaques with white numbers for runs scored under the appropriate innings and getting cracked bats for my work. The bats would be put back together with black electricians' tape and traded with friends in exchange for marbles, bottles of Coke, or a comic book.

What a gift the open, awesome St. John's campus was for a Main Street boy, and I spent many wonderful hours there, including time spent bouncing lacrosse balls off the World War I monument at the campus entrance. The monument, honoring St. John's students who were killed in the First World War, features a bronze inlay of Lady Liberty encased in cement. The erratic bounces of my lacrosse balls off the bas-relief, bronze lady honed my skills at running down the wayward bounces of the hard rubber ball. I hope it wouldn't have bothered the two dozen heroes whose names were enshrined on the reverse side.

The entrance walk off College Avenue went by the monument straight up to McDowell Hall. Some of my hours at St. John's were spent lounging in the basement of McDowell Hall, the main campus building and an historic treasure, the centerpiece of this educational facility that dates to 1696 with the founding of King Williams School, the first "free school" in America. Don't be fooled by the term "free school." Children did not attend free of charge; "free school" simply meant that the students received a liberating education. The St. Johns' College motto says it well: "Facio Liberos Ex Liberis Libris Libraque." [I make free men from children with books and a balance.]

The school was named for King William, England's monarch, and it started in a small school house built on State Circle in Annapolis.

St. John's College, probably named in honor of St. John the Evangelist, was chartered by the State of Maryland in 1784. Soon thereafter, King Williams School was consolidated into the college. Four of the college's founders were the Maryland signers of the Declaration of Independence, and each served on its first Board of Governors. Charles Carroll of Carrolton contributed the largest sum to the founding of the college—200 pounds—and William Paca, then the state's governor, by his signature made the charter law.

The state also gave the college a building called "Bladen's folly," a partially built governor's mansion begun in 1744 by Governor Thomas Bladen but abandoned amid political disagreements. The building, completed 50 years after its start, was named after the college's first president, John McDowell. This magnificent, three-story colonial structure, originally housed the students and classrooms. In my day, it held mostly offices with a grand hall upstairs, but my refuge in inclement weather, the need for a lavatory, or a rest from athletics, was the basement lounge.

The outside brick steps down to the basement led me to cushioned sofas and chairs and reading material. They weren't "great books," but it was a great place to spend some quiet hours. It piqued my interest in the bookish side of college. While many Annapolis "Townies" viewed the untraditional "Johnnies," with their flare for unconventional dress and hairstyles, as affected aesthetes, I found them to be bright and friendly to a youthful interloper. In fact, later I would realize they were much like other college kids, perhaps smarter than most.

Francis Scott Key

I didn't think of it then, but those basement rooms in McDowell Hall are very meaningful to American history because they must have been used by some early, illustrious students, including St. John's most famous graduate, Francis Scott Key. Key spent seven years at St. John's, enrolling in the grammar school at age 10 when St. John's opened its doors in November 1789. He lived with his great aunt and uncle Dr. and Mrs. Upton Scott from whom Francis derived his middle name, at their mansion on Shipwright Street, near the Charles Carroll of Carrolton home. (The Scott house was very familiar to me since it stood across the street from the home of good friends and the apartment where my future wife would live before our marriage.) When Key graduated in 1796, he was chosen valedictory orator of the class.

Born in Frederick, Md., Key could be considered something of an Annapolitan since he lived in the city until he was 21, studying law in town after college under the guidance of an esteemed uncle and eventually marrying in the Chase-Lloyd House. (An interesting sidelight: Key and Roger Brooke Taney studied law in Annapolis at the same time, and they became lifelong friends. Taney would marry Key's sister Anne.)

Among Key's classmates were two nephews of President George Washington, who came to visit them at the college in 1791 and undoubtedly impressed a student such as Key, a romantic and patriotic youth very much taken with the Revolutionary history in Annapolis. Key also became a great friend of his college mate John Shaw, son of the famous cabinet-maker. The younger Shaw bonded with Key over their mutual love of reading and writing poetry, a love that would eventually gain Key everlasting fame.

Soon after Key married Mary Tayloe Lloyd in the Chase-Lloyd House, the couple moved to Washington, D.C., where Francis set up his law practice. He was there in 1814 when the British invaded Washington, burning the White House and the Capitol. The British generals used the plantation of Dr. William Beanes as headquarters and later, questioning his allegiance, imprisoned Beanes on one of their ships in the Baltimore Harbor. Francis Scott Key, who was a good friend of Beanes, went to Baltimore to ask for his release. The British agreed but forced Key and Beanes to stay on their ship in the Baltimore harbor so they could not give away the British positions preparing the attack on Baltimore's Fort McHenry. In the morning, when Key gazed on the American Flag still flying over the fort after a night of bombardment, his poetic and patriotic nature took flight and he wrote the verses of what became "The Star-Spangled Banner," a poem first titled "Defence of Fort McHenry." When the poem was published, Key directed it be sung to the tune of "To Anacreon in Heaven," a British melody well known in America.

Many years later, the then U.S. Chief Justice Taney said the "The Star-Spangled Banner" revealed his brother-in-law's "genius and taste as a poet" and the "warm spirit of patriotism which breathes in the song." The U.S. Congress agreed with the latter sentiment in 1931 when it made Key's song the National Anthem.

On my visits to St. John's, I spent some time where I know both Key and Washington tarried—under the "Liberty Tree." On one side of the green entering the college stood a great tulip poplar estimated to be 400 years old. I tried to wrap my arms around its trunk and got less than a fifth of the way. The tree was 20 feet in circumference and 100 feet high and was known as the "Liberty

Tree" because the Sons of Liberty supposedly met there in 1775 to plot the revolution. Later events under the tree included Lafayette's review of the Maryland Militia in 1824 during his invitational visit to Annapolis. (Sadly, the "Liberty Tree" was irreparably damaged by Hurricane Floyd in 1999 and had to be removed.)

This 400-year-old tulip poplar, 100 feet high and 20 feet in circumference, graced the front lawn at St. John's throughout the college's history, spreading its branches over many graduations as well as such visiting luminaries as George Washington and, supposedly, the revolution-plotting "Sons of Liberty," which gave the tree its name. Sadly, the 1999 hurricane "Floyd" irreparably damaged the tree. (Courtesy of M.E. Warren Photography, LLC)

The Great Books vs. the Navy

The college adopted the study of the great books of Western

Civilization in 1937.   When I was a youth, St. John's became synonymous with "The Great Books" curriculum.   Having abolished military training in 1923, St. John's became more conventional and less successful, and when the depression hit, it couldn't meet operating expenses.   In 1936, St. John's lost its accreditation.   In desperation, the College Board brought in two innovative academics, Stringfellow Barr and Scott Buchanan, who revolutionized the curriculum and turned the little Annapolis school into a world-renowned liberal arts college.   Based on the 100 great books selected by Barr, the "new program," as it was originally called, demanded that students read and discuss original works in philosophy, theology, mathematics, science, music, poetry and literature.   Francis Scott Key would have approved.   By the time Buchanan and Barr took over, the campus had grown from its original four acres to 32 acres.   Desire for those acres by the college's neighbor, the Naval Academy, almost caused the demise of St. John's.

In the mid-1940s, with the country just ending the Second World War, the Naval Academy wanted more space for its growing officer training needs. I remember my parents talking about it at the dinner table, somewhat fearfully discussing what might happen to dad's job if the Academy was moved to California, as some of that state's congressmen proposed, touting the unlimited space available. The concern that the Academy acquiring St. John's would increase dad's workload was far outweighed by economic considerations. Everyone in Annapolis whose livelihood depended on the millions of dollars spent in Annapolis because of the Academy, employees and merchants alike, had similar fears.   Thus, the Academy's annexation of St. John's property was supported by residents, politicians, Navy grads, the local paper, and even the Maryland General Assembly. That is understandable. In the mid-1940s, the Naval Academy was the foundation of Annapolis' viability as a city. In fact, "Annapolis" and "The Naval Academy" had become synonymous to outsiders. Congress, which had the eventual say, at first supported the Academy. Eventually, a "Save St. John's campaign," other options for training naval officers (NROTC) and the idea of reclaiming land from the Severn River caused Congress to reverse itself, thus saving St. John's.

One battle between St. John's and the Naval Academy remains. Earlier, I mentioned St. John's demise as an athletic power, but there's one caveat to that. Each year for more than 30 years St. Johnnies, dressed in fun, eclectic clothing, have a game against the midshipmen from across the street, in their military uniforms. The conflict—croquet. St. John's has bested its Navy foe 80% of the time.

The traditional croquet match between the Midshipmen of Navy and the St. Johnnies draws large crowds every year. (Courtesy of the U.S. Naval Academy Special Collections and Archives)

CHAPTER TWELVE

AN EVEN MORE UNIQUE PLAYGROUND

THE U. S. NAVAL ACADEMY

The Naval Academy was an integral part of my childhood. In fact, my mother walked me there in a baby carriage, and I crawled around on the grassy lawn in front of the Academy's Chapel with its green copper dome.

It was an easy walk for my mother to push me in my stroller (as I'm shown here) from Main Street to the Naval Academy.

My mother told the tale of sitting on a bench, reading by my carriage one summer day, looking high up the Chapel dome, some 200 feet in the air, to see my father hanging on a rope-held seat repairing the copper roof. She hightailed it home and would return only with the guarantee my father wasn't working on the dome that day.

I recall as a toddler the joy of being on the Chapel green frolicking to the sounds of the Chapel bells, and picking up chestnuts fallen from the trees, peeling off the skins to reveal the smooth chocolate brown nuts. They made great missiles to throw at the trees. The Chapel, called the "Cathedral of the Navy," holds many memories, from visits to John Paul Jones' crypt in the basement to the enormously long walk down the aisle with my oldest daughter, Laura, at her wedding. My family often went to Christmas midnight mass at the Chapel, and I would accompany them. On one such very cold and snowy Christmas Eve, as I went to get the car while my family waited atop the long set of stairs to the Chapel door, a young Navy doctor named John Avallone spotted Laura and, with a "Wow, who is that?," he wangled an introduction. Two days after Christmas two years later, I walked Laura down the incredibly long Chapel aisle to wed John Avallone.

The U.S. Naval Academy Chapel, called the "Cathedral of the Navy," holds many memories for my family—from my dad's work on the dome to my daughter's wedding there.

How the remains of John Paul Jones, America's greatest Revolutionary War Naval hero, came to rest in the Academy Chapel starts with Winston Churchill's book, *Richard Carvel* and unfolds like a great mystery and adventure novel. John Paul Jones is portrayed in the 1899 novel as a hero who rescues the main character, Richard Carvel, from pirates. In the novel, Richard eventually returns to Annapolis, but later joins Jones' crew aboard the *Bonhomme Richard*, the ship Jones commanded in 1779 where he refused to surrender to the British, supposedly uttering the now famous Navy slogan, "I have not yet begun to fight." The novel piqued the interest of U.S. Army General Horace Porter, America's Ambassador to France at the time, in finding Jones' unknown resting place. Jones had died in Paris in 1792 and been buried in a forgotten grave, in an obscure cemetery that was later paved over. After a five-year search, in 1905 the body was found under a laundry on the outskirts of Paris, in a lead casket filled with alcohol, preserving it and making identification possible. A squadron of American warships escorted the body to America and to its last resting place at the Naval Academy, where it was greeted by President Theodore Roosevelt.

John Paul Jones, known as "Father of the U.S. Navy," was buried in this ornate crypt in the Academy Chapel after an unusual search for his remains in Paris, France. (Courtesy of the U.S. Naval Academy Special Collections and Archives)

It took seven years after the arrival of Jones remains for Congress to appropriate the money to finish the ornate Chapel Crypt inside a sarcophagus made of some 20 tons of marble columns. During those seven years, the casket remained on trestles, which led irreverent midshipmen to parody the popular 1905 song, "Everybody Works but Father," in which a son laments that he and his mother work all day while his father just lounges around. The parody:

Everybody works but John Paul Jones!
He lies around all day,
Body pickled in alcohol
On a permanent jag, they say.
Middies stand around him
Doing honor to his bones;
Everybody works in "Crabtown"
But John Paul Jones!

"Crabtown," of course, is a nickname for Annapolis, especially used by midshipmen, as several of their sports fight songs attest. The most popular of these songs is called "The Service Boast," a challenge to Army's football team. It goes:

Oh, you've heard of the Navy and the men who sail the seas
For the glory of our country's colors fair.
For the glory of the Blue and Gold our team is here today,
And we'll cheer them as through Army's line they tear.
Oh, there'll be high elation on the far China Station,
From Crabtown to ships at Timbuctoo,
And we'll drink a merry toast to our team, the Service boast,
And the wearers of the good old Navy blue.

Of course, many midshipmen see Annapolis as an appendage of the Academy, as humorously described in "Midshipman Lingo:" "N. Annapolis, a fishing village on the banks of the Naval Academy."

(We also used to call the *Evening Capital*, our local paper, the "Crabwrapper." In truth, that's accurate, since we often ate crabs off of spread out newspapers, making the shells and waste easy to wrap when finished.)

Annapolis = Naval Academy

The Academy transformed Annapolis from the sleepy little

town it had become after Baltimore supplanted it as the port city of Maryland. As mentioned earlier, the Academy and Annapolis literally became synonymous. Often, when I told strangers I was from Annapolis, they'd say, "Oh, you're in the Navy." This correlating identity was fostered when movies and books about the Academy were given an "Annapolis" title, such as two 1937 motion pictures "Annapolis Salute" and "Navy Blue and Gold: The Love Story of Annapolis," not to mention several since.

With its colonial prominence faded and its port value diminished, Annapolis was revitalized in 1845 when it was chosen as the site for the training school for naval officers. John Paul Jones had suggested such a school in his day, as had others, but the prevailing thought in Jones' day was that naval men should not be trained anywhere but at sea. However, the introduction of steam propulsion and the screw propeller in the 1830s made engineering knowledge a necessity. Enter George Bancroft, who became Secretary of the Navy in early 1845. Bancroft chose Annapolis for the site of the naval school mainly because of the presence of Fort Severn, an outdated Army installation that overlooked the Severn River where it meets Spa Creek, on land the government already owned.

An aerial view of the U.S. Naval Academy, which covers 340 acres between the Severn River (top) and boat-filled Spa Creek (bottom). The Annapolis city dock and the Eastport bridge can be seen (lower left), and North Severn (near the original Puritan's Providence settlement) at the top across the Severn. (Courtesy of the U.S. Naval Academy Special Collections and Archives)

From its original 10 acres, the Academy grew to the present 340 acres, by annexing some of Hell Point, at the foot of King George Street near City Dock and dredging more than 60 acres of silt from the Severn River and Spa Creek into steel bulkheads along the shore. The latter concept helped erase the potential grab of St. John's campus. In my day, as the Academy impacted Annapolis, the town influenced its midshipmen. A midshipman grown to officer put it best. In an article titled "Annapolis, Mother of Navy Men" in the October, 1935 U.S. Naval Institute Proceedings, then Lieutenant Arthur A. Ageton, talked of the City's value of the historic charm and "air of aristocratic sufficiency" to midshipmen. He wrote:

> *And even now, when one enters those historic homes, one finds the same courtesy and gentility which marked them in an older day. This is of much importance to the Naval Academy, for the midshipmen in their daily and weekly liberties, in their social life, in all their activities outside the white walls of the Academy, are influenced and molded by this more ancient culture, which is not so much evidenced by deed and word as it is absorbed in the very atmosphere of the town.*

As the Academy grew so did the employment of locals such as my father, grandfather and assorted uncles. In my youth, one out of four Annapolitan males worked at the Academy, not to mention the impact of naval personnel on real estate, tailors, restaurants and other local businesses.

As I grew older, this sprawling military college campus became even more central to my life and those of many of my peers. The fact that my dad worked there, and I even considered attending the Academy, suffused it in my everyday existence. But even more involving for my generation was the entertainment the Academy offered continuously—band concerts, parades, visiting ships and dignitaries, sports galore, and prime college facilities at our disposal.

A weekend or summer's day might include swinging on the rings, jumping on the gymnastic horse, or trying to handstand on the parallel bars in Macdonough Hall, the Academy's one-time boathouse that became a gymnasium. We'd play tennis on the bright red clay courts overlooking the Severn. If we carried a basketball to the Academy, we would play on the Navy team's courts in Dahlgren Hall, the former Armory and drill area; turned into the varsity basketball arena, until the "Jimmy Legs" (an ancient, nautical nickname applied to Academy guards) would shoo us out; then we'd play on the outdoor courts beside Dahlgren. Or we might sneak into "Smoke Hall," a midshipmen recreation center in Bancroft Hall, for a game of pool.

Dahlgren Hall is the site of another Academy tradition, the Ring Dance, when midshipmen (we called them "mids") received their class rings signifying they are wedded to the Navy. Navy Chaplains gather water from around the world for the occasion, and the mids ceremoniously dip their rings in these waters from the seven seas. The Ring Dance is one of the many "hops" for mids in their dress blues to escort young ladies, called "Hop Girls" or "Drags," to the Academy. These occasions were also an opportunity for local young men, including me in my early college years, to "late date" the mids' dates. At around 11 p.m. when some mids had to rush back to the Academy for curfew, we'd head for Carvel Hall, where some of these "Drags" stayed, and a chance for a late evening pizza with a willing young lady.

One year, when I was 12 or 13, my parents decided to take advantage of the opportunity to rent rooms to the drags during "June Week," the Academy's graduation week. They rented my bedroom, their room and the living room to three young ladies. We slept in makeshift beds in the dining room. I was quite taken with these girls. They seemed glamorous "women" to me. They were probably 20 at the most. It was my first up close experience with the opposite sex, and I was agog with sexual wonderment, especially when one girl left the bathroom when the dining room door was open. She was in a slip that the light passed through revealing some shapely legs. Six or seven years later, I would be late-dating similar young ladies.

Bancroft's Vision

If I was on my own at the Academy, I'd often go to the basement of Bancroft Hall, through the many corridors and make my way to the sheet metal shop for a visit with my father and his shop mates, who always gave me a loud, vocal greeting as "Hinky's" son. Those Bancroft Hall visits were always pleasing because my dad was held in such high esteem by his coworkers, and it showed in the way they fondly kidded him. He would become the shop boss one day, a position that drove him to retirement, as I mentioned earlier.

Dad's talent with metalworking had its culinary rewards as well as its sports equipment trade value. The bakery in Bancroft Hall's basement often needed mixing bowls or utensil repairs, which Dad did willingly. He was usually rewarded with a cake or pie, which he often brought home. I will never forget the fresh strawberry pie, with its huge red strawberries topped with bakery-made whipped cream, he would produce from his tool box several times a year. I've never met its delicious match.

All Academy employees were treated to a picnic each year when I was a youngster. We'd take the yard patrol boats from the Academy across the Severn to Greenbury Point for a day of games and treats, such as hot dogs and soft drinks. About that time, occasionally we'd see a seaplane taking off or landing on the Severn, a scary sight for some boaters on the river.

Greenbury Point was also the site of the Navy's first Air Station, opened in 1911, and using planes bought from air flight pioneers the Wright Brothers and Glenn Curtiss, Navy pilots set records for air time and altitude over the Bay. They also successfully tested the first compressed air catapult to launch a plane from a ship.

Annapolis lost naval air in 1913 when the need for more air field space and year-round good weather led to a move to Florida and the birth of the Pensacola Naval Air Station.

Called the world's largest stand-alone college dormitory, Bancroft Hall, shown here over the Tecumseh statue's shoulder, houses all 4,000 midshipmen and operates like a city in one building. (Courtesy of the U.S. Naval Academy Special Collections and Archives)

Bancroft Hall was a magical place, almost a city under one roof. It's called the world's largest stand-alone college dormitory, housing more than 4,000 midshipmen in 1,800 rooms, with 4.8 miles of corridors and 33 acres of floor space. Bancroft Hall is one of 27 buildings constructed at the Academy between 1900 and 1910. Ten of them, including the Chapel, formed the most outstanding group of Beaux-Arts buildings in the United States. They were designed by New York architect Ernest Flagg, then America's primary proponent of the Beaux-Arts style. "Beaux-Arts" expresses the neoclassical French style that influenced architecture in the U.S. between 1880 and 1920, especially in college and government buildings. One of its features, the Mansard Roof, is a defining detail of many Academy structures. Among the Beaux-Arts buildings also were the homes on "Captain's Row," built in 1905 to house the Academy's ranking officers.

A high school friend of mine lived on Captain's Row, actually named Porter Road, a block full of houses which, in my day, were just inside Gate One near Thompson Stadium.

Visiting my friend at his house was an awesome experience for a Main Street kid living in a third floor apartment. I couldn't believe the grandeur of the home. I believe you could fit our whole apartment in the enormous basement where my friend and I played ping pong. Everywhere you looked were fireplaces and carved wood moldings, and two ornate staircases led upstairs. I later learned the size of the houses, at least 8,000 square feet, with 12-foot ceilings on the main floor. The only home larger was the Academy Superintendent's quarters, to which I was invited later in life because of my position as President of the Annapolis Chamber of Commerce. Known now as "Buchanan House," the "Supe's" quarters, also a Beaux-Arts style mansion, sits next to the Chapel. It is named after Admiral Franklin Buchanan, the Academy's first superintendent, who ably carried out George Bancroft's vision for starting the naval school.

The original granite-grey buildings that dominate the Academy grounds always impressed me. Many had metal roofs or ornamental elements that gave the grey a greenish tint—and also provided lots of work for my dad and the sheet metal shop crew.

(A personal digression: I recall seeing my dad, tools in hand, walking along the high, pitched roof of Dahlgren Hall as I headed inside to play basketball with friends. I envied his fearlessness but knew then that walking roofs was not for me.

As a teenager, I was ambivalent about my dad's job. On the one hand, I was proud of his affable, high standing among his peers and his leadership without trying to lead in the sheet metal shop. On the other hand, I was a bit embarrassed of his working man status and seeming lack of ambition when I was among friends whose fathers were naval officers, business owners and doctors.

Yet, as I grew into manhood, I began to appreciate how reliable and friendly my dad was and how he had overcome a difficult childhood to become a steady hand and provider for my mom and me. And, as the years went by, and I dealt daily with less affable, less friendly men, I began to appreciate him even more. I often wished I had his temperament.)

Back to Bancroft Hall:

Everything from bank to barber shop is located in this grand building the mids call, "Mother B." It even has its own zip code.

In Bancroft Hall's dining room, King Hall, 4,000 midshipmen all eat together at the same time. (Courtesy of the U.S. Naval Academy Special Collections and Archives)

Perhaps Bancroft Hall's most unusual room is King Hall, where all the midshipmen are fed, simultaneously, three meals a day. In my adult years, as a Navy tennis booster, I ate several times in King Hall with the mids. Sitting with fellow boosters at one of the long dining tables in this three-football-fields-in-size room, you could feel the floor shake when suddenly, like someone opened a series of human spigots, 4,000 plus hungry young mids descended on the mess hall, gathering at their assigned tables, and devouring heaping plates of food in about half an hour. While the meal was a respite for most mids, it could be daunting for plebes (freshmen). The plebes sat bolt upright on the edge of their seats, and some had to "eat a square meal," bringing fork to mouth in an exaggerated motion straight up from their plates and horizontally to their mouths. Some plebes had to answer innocuous questions for which there were stock answers they must memorize. For example:

> **Upper Classman Question**: "How long have you been in the Navy, mister?"

> **Plebe Answer**: "All me bloomin' life, sir! Me mother was a mermaid; me father was King Neptune. I was born on the crest of a wave and rocked in the cradle of the deep. Seaweed and barnacles are me clothes. Every tooth in me head is a marlinspike; the hair on me head is hemp. Every bone in me body is a spar and when I spits, I spits tar. I'm hard, I is, I am, I are, sir!"

Having dined with the brigade a few times, I can guarantee the mids ate very well—especially if dessert was strawberry pie.

God of 2.0

Facing Bancroft Hall is a monument beloved by most midshipmen, the bust of Tecumseh, called the "God of 2.0," the Academy's passing grade in my youth. I loved it, too, as a youngster, because when the mids prayed for good test grades or a win over Army, they threw pennies at their good luck charm, Tecumseh, as they marched by, and we kids gathered the pennies as if it was an Easter egg hunt. Tecumseh is a large, bronze Indian's upper torso, a replica of the original wooden figurehead of the USS Delaware from Civil War days. Before Navy's games against Army, what fun it was to see Tecumseh covered in war paint, his face streaked with red, green, yellow and white with multi-colored arrows in his bronze quiver.

Tecumseh is one of several monuments that grace the greenway in front of Bancroft Hall. The most fun these monuments produced occurred each spring as we watched plebes try to climb the Herndon obelisk, a 21-foot high column sometimes slathered with lard, literally a granite greased pig, and crown it with a "Dixie Cup" cap worn by plebes. It's a hilarious scene watching dozens of plebes form a human pyramid to boost one member high enough to replace the Dixie Cup cap on top with a traditional midshipman's hat, ceremoniously transforming plebes to upper classmen. Though Herndon has been climbed in minutes, it usually took a couple of hours, providing us onlookers many slips, falls and progress to laugh at or cheer. Tradition has it that whichever plebe replaces the cap is destined to become the class's first admiral.

The bronze statue of a ship's figurehead, the Indian Chief Tecumseh puts on his war paint for the Army-Navy football game. (Courtesy of the U.S. Naval Academy Special Collections and Archives)

Like most Academy monuments, Herndon was named for a Naval hero, in this case for a 19th century sea captain, William Herndon, who amid a ferocious hurricane, transferred 152 passengers and crewmen safely to a rescue ship, then changed into a full dress uniform and returned to the bridge to go down with his ship. My favorite monument is the one honoring Stephen Decatur, a native Marylander, the youngest man to reach the rank of captain in the Navy's history. The hero of several wars and sea battles, his monument contains four of the guns of the British Frigate *HMS Macedonian*, which Decatur captured in the War of 1812. Decatur brought the Macedonian back to the U.S., the first British warship ever brought into an American harbor. The monument also has concrete benches attached, which makes it special for me. Mom, Dad and I often would travel to the Academy for various events. We documented two of these trips with photos that remain among my most nostalgic possessions, photos of my dad and me on the Decatur monument benches, me standing on the bench with dad standing in front, when I was three and he was 35, and a repeat, with me sitting and dad standing, when I was 21 and he was 54, a composite of years together in a familiar playground, the Naval Academy.

A time capsule of my dad and me at the Naval Academy. On the left when I was three and dad was 35; on the right, a repeat photo when dad was 54 and I was 21.

If Tecumseh brought victory over Army in football, we young Annapolitans would be sure to head for the Academy when the mids returned from Philadelphia following the game. We'd go to watch Navy's football players ring the Japanese bell in victory. The Japanese bell, real name "Gokokuji" bell, was a 1456 casting given to Admiral Matthew Perry following his 1855 expedition to Japan. At Perry's death in 1858, his widow honored his request that the bell be given to the Naval Academy. (The original bell was returned to the people of Okinawa in 1987. A replica has been rung since then.) The mids were exuberant at the bell-ringing because nothing excited them more than a football victory over Army, and as an unabashed Navy fan in my youth, Navy football became an ongoing passion.

Chapter Thirteen

Navy Football, Friends and Heroes

One of the great sanctums in Academy lore was Thompson Field, the Navy football stadium of my youth. It was a small grass field surrounded by a track, with bleachers on both sides, and room for additional seats at the end zones. One end zone was so close to Spa Creek that the ball kicked for an extra point could bounce into the water. The field sat just inside Academy Gate One, at the end of King George Street, and it stoked my youthful dream of athletic prowess. I believe I first entered this field of dreams in 1942, when my dad took me to the most unique of all Army-Navy games.

Because of World War II, it was decreed that neither the mids nor cadets of Army could travel by vehicle or train, so the game was scheduled for Thompson Field, with the West Point team travelling by boat from the Hudson to the Severn. It was also decreed that only locals living within 10 miles of the Academy could attend the game. Even First Lady Eleanor Roosevelt couldn't attend because she lived in Washington, D.C.

My dad got two tickets for the game, but at $4.40 a piece I'm sure he wouldn't spend that much money for a football contest. I guess he either got tickets from one of his brothers-in-law, who worked with the Navy Athletic Association, or traded some metalwork—a copper pot, a lamp, or some metal utensil—for a pair. (Dad was always doing metalworking favors for friends, family or fellow employees. He made them some wonderful flower pots and planters, and, when I went off to college, he made me a metal lamp that fit over my bed headboard, lighting many a late evening's studying in bed.)

For this unlikely chance to attend an Army-Navy game in Annapolis, I can envision dad and me walking down Main Street, joining some of my friends, such as John Henneberger, who recalls being there, and their fathers in the short trek to Thompson Field. I faintly remember the game, though those memories could mix with the many games I attended there as a Boy Scout, selling programs in exchange for free entry (and scouring under the stands for dropped programs we could resell and pocket the cash). At any rate, because the corps of cadets was not allowed to travel to the 1942 game, the third- and fourth-class midshipmen were ordered to sit behind the Army bench and cheer for the cadets. Navy won this unusual game 14-0, and most of its participants would soon find themselves fighting a war, a number of whom would die in battle.

I actually got to play on Thompson Field once as a youngster when a ragtag bunch of locals challenged a team of "Navy Juniors," the sons of coaches and officers stationed at the Academy. We showed up in our street clothes, with a few helmets, fewer cleats and no uniforms. The "Navy Juniors" ran onto the field in complete Navy blue and gold uniforms, helmets, cleats and all. It was enough to intimidate me, but not a bunch of "Hell Pointers" on our team. They were as tough as the oyster shells their fathers harvested. Despite their hard-hitting efforts, we lost the game to the passing of a quarterback I was told was the son of Tom Hamilton, Navy's football coach and onetime Navy All-American halfback. (It was the elder Coach Hamilton who, when his 1-8 Navy team, trailing undefeated Army 21-18, and driving for the end zone, eschewed a game-tying-field-goal, justified his decision with the immortal words, "a tie is like kissing your sister.")

Barnacle Bill

My dad's favorite Navy football player was another All-American halfback named Bill Busik. A three-sport star at Navy, Busik is remembered most for his exploits in the 1941 Army-Navy game, where he single-handedly punted, passed and rushed Navy to a 14-6 victory. He also played safety on defense.

William S. Busik led an exceptional life, back to his high school days in California when he shared a backfield, a baseball diamond, a track and a basketball court with a teammate and friend who would become an even more famous athlete—Jackie Robinson, who broke the color barrier in major league baseball. "In baseball, I was the second baseman and he was the shortstop," Bill Busik once explained his teaming with Robinson. "We were both long jumpers in track. In basketball, he was a forward, and I was a guard. In football, when I was at fullback, he was the tailback."

Following his early graduation from the Naval Academy due to the war, Bill Busik was stationed aboard the USS Shaw, a destroyer that fought in the Pacific. While he sat in a gun director's deck sixty

feet above the water directing fire at enemy planes, the Shaw was
hit by a bomb, and Busik was thrown from his perch only to be
saved by a guide wire that wrapped around his leg. The whole saga
is detailed in a chapter called "Barnacle Bill," Busik's nickname, in
Lars Anderson's book *The All Americans*. The nickname came from
the old sea ditty: "He's rough and tough and knows his stuff; he's
Barnacle Bill the sailor."

Midshipman William S. Busik, class of 1943, in his football gear. (Courtesy of
the U.S. Naval Academy Special Collections and Archives)

Busik retired from the Navy in 1971, having topped off his
career as director of athletics at Navy. After retirement, he returned
to Annapolis to live, and he became executive director of the Naval
Academy Athletic Association, which is when I first met him. We
were just acquaintances until around 1990 when he called me to
ask if I would help him promote "First Night Annapolis," a family
oriented, alcohol-free celebration on New Year's Eve, of which he
was chairman.

When we met for lunch to discuss First Night, I mentioned that
he had been my father's favorite Navy player. Bill only smiled and
nodded as he must have so many times when his football exploits
were lauded. I remember him in those days, still standing arrow-
straight, fit and handsome in his 70s, a self-effacing gentleman, in
every sense of the word. We often expect our sports heroes to be
guides in life, though they seldom are. But Bill Busik displayed his
heroic and team-oriented loyalty throughout his life.

Father Jake

Midshipman John Francis Laboon, Jr.'s graduation picture, class of 1944, before his World War II heroics. (Courtesy of the U.S. Naval Academy Special Collections and Archives)

Loyalty is a deep-seated value among those who attend the Academy, especially its athletes. Such loyalty leads me to another Navy hero who played football with Bill Busik, one of his star blockers, John Francis Laboon, Jr. For example, in a 1941 game "Jake" Laboon knocked out a Penn player who had taken out Bill Busik with a cheap, illegal hit. It's a trifling example, because Jake Laboon would display much more devotion to country, Navy and his fellow man in the years after football.

I was partial to Jake Laboon for many reasons, one being that he was also a lacrosse player, an All-American defenseman on Navy's 1943 National Championship team. While his time at the Academy was marked by athletic and academic accomplishment, Jake would go on to greater glories. An accelerated graduate in 1943, he trained as a submarine officer and was assigned to the USS Peto, a sub patrolling Pacific waters.

During one war patrol, the Peto picked up a downed American

pilot and searched for his downed wingman, who was spotted in shallow, mined water near a Japanese held island. Since the sub couldn't maneuver closer for fear of grounding and coming in range of enemy fire from a Japanese shore battery, the Peto's captain asked for a volunteer to make a swimming rescue. Without hesitation, Jake Laboon volunteered. The athletic Jake, with a rope tied around his waist, swam through the mined waters with bullets splashing around him and brought the airman to safety. For his bravery, the then Lieutenant Junior Grade John Francis Laboon was awarded the prestigious Silver Star.

Lieutenant Laboon resigned from the Navy shortly after the end of World War II and entered the Jesuit order. He was ordained a Jesuit priest in 1956 and, as a Naval Reservist, he was recalled to active duty and served as a battlefield chaplain in Vietnam, where he was awarded a combat "V" for his fearless support of injured troops. Toward the end of his career, "Father Jake," as he came to be known, became Senior Catholic Chaplain at the Naval Academy, and after his 1980 retirement, returned to Annapolis to oversee construction at the Jesuit retreat facility, Manresa-on-Severn, from whose high perch on the river you could see the Academy.

"Father Jake" Laboon presides over the marriage of my daughter Laura to Navy doctor John Avallone in the Academy Chapel.

It was "Father Jake" who stood on the altar awaiting my

daughter, Laura, as she and I walked down that long aisle in the Naval Academy Chapel on her wedding day in December, 1986. His admonition to Laura at the end of the ceremony, "Laura, it's your duty to be a good Navy wife," was typical Jake, always loyal to the Navy. As noted earlier, Laura was marrying John Avallone, a Navy doctor whose family was very friendly with Father Jake. John's dad, Gene Avallone, was also an Academy graduate and submariner, and he and his wife Nancy were devoted supporters of the Chapel and the priests, often entertaining them for dinner at home. That's where I first met Father Jake, at the Avallone's, and I must admit, I was most interested in him as a lacrosse player— until I heard of his heroism. That heroism led to the naming of the destroyer USS Laboon after Jake, as well as the Laboon Chaplain's Center at the Naval Academy.

I became friendly with several Navy sports heroes later in life. Like Bill Busik, they were drawn back to Annapolis by the Academy. One I watched play in the war years of 1943-45, was Henry Richard Duden, Jr., probably the greatest multi-sport athlete I have seen personally. "Dick" Duden was an All-American end on Navy's 1945 7-1-1 team, which he captained. I also watched him excel in baseball and basketball, winning nine varsity letters at Navy. Winner of the Knute Rockne award given by the Touchdown Club of Washington, D.C., as the nation's best lineman, Dick was awarded the USNA sword as the Navy's top athlete when he graduated. After service in the fleet from 1946 to 1949, Dick played one year of professional football with the New York Giants before being called back to active duty during the Korean War.

Dick returned to Annapolis to operate his insurance business and coach the Navy plebe football team. Dick was a founding member of the Annapolis Touchdown Club and served as its president, a post I would also hold later. Dick and I became friendly through our Touchdown Club connections, other local organizations and at mutual friends' parties. Dick was "Hail fellow, well met" personified, jovial and affable and without ego. When his sports success were brought up, Dick always defected praise to his teammates. His son Jason played lacrosse with my son, Ray. His son Dick, a lacrosse player too, also became a friend of our family. The younger Dick married the daughter of a childhood friend of mine, the small town intermingling of friends and relatives seen at work once more.

I also had the pleasure of knowing another Navy sports hero, this one of a different ilk—a sailor, in the absolute meaning of the word. I knew him as Bob, a fellow board member at Annapolis

Bank and Trust. He was Rear Admiral Robert W. McNitt, a war hero of some merit, with two Silver Stars to his credit. During World War II, Bob was executive officer of the submarine USS Barb, credited with sinking 29 Japanese ships. When Bob and I became friends, he was the first civilian dean of admissions at the Naval Academy.

Navy three sports star, Henry Richard "Dick" Duden, Jr., a 1945 football All American, returned to Annapolis to live and work and also coach at Navy.

(Courtesy of the U.S. Naval Academy Special Collections and Archives)

Navy sailing star and future admiral, Midshipman Robert W. McNitt's graduation picture, class of 1938. (Courtesy of the U.S. Naval Academy Special Collections and Archives)

A lover of sailboat racing, Bob McNitt is credited with establishing the Academy's ocean sailing program as Vice Chairman of the Midshipmen Boat Club in 1937. He talked the Academy administration into entering the *Vamarie*, a 72-foot sailing yacht given as a gift to the Academy, in the prestigious annual Newport to Bermuda ocean race. Of course, a crew member on that first race was Midshipman McNitt. The Academy has participated in every biannual Bermuda race since then.

Navy sports heroes are not the only celebrities that I have met in my time. As a young journalist, I interviewed an elderly Eleanor Roosevelt in Baltimore; interviewed Robert Kennedy soon after his brother, President John Kennedy, named him U.S. Attorney General; chatted with Lyndon Johnson in the White House; interviewed Wally Shirra the day after he was selected as one of the original seven Mercury Astronauts, and interviewed many congressmen and cabinet members as a Washington correspondent. Yet the person I most admired was a Naval Academy man, Captain Edward A. Shuman III, better known as "Ned," a Navy flyer who spent 1,824 days in captivity as a Viet Cong Prisoner of War.

My Hero—Ned Shuman

I first met Ned when I was invited to play in the regular poker game at the Annapolis Yacht Club, which sits on Spa Creek next to the Eastport Bridge in sight of the Naval Academy. A crusty, sometimes profane card player, Ned also had that loyalty gene.

Ned and I bonded over my becoming a member of the Yacht Club. When the poker players suggested I join the Club, I doubted my eligibility, since I was neither sailor nor power boater, the main criteria for membership. Ned proposed me to the membership committee, and in response to the expected complaint, "He's not a boater," Ned replied: "He sails with me." Ned then came to me and said, "Let's go sailing." So, for the first time, I joined Ned on his sailboat, sailing out of his dock on Weems Creek into the Severn River, around the Naval Academy, with the Chesapeake Bay before us, and into Spa Creek, past the City Dock to the Yacht Club for lunch. Needless to say, I was elected to membership in the Club.

Ned and I travelled together to a casino in Atlantic City, had dinner with our wives and poker friends at the Yacht Club, and ate lunch occasionally at a little German restaurant called Regina's near my office and his home. I'd often ask him about his five years as a POW, and beyond mentions of his lifetime pass to all major league baseball games, and those cursed trips to get his annual POW physical, he didn't elaborate. The one time he opened up a bit was when I asked him about an event he experienced about which his fellow POW and Medal of Honor winner Leo Thorsness, in his book *Surviving Hell*, said: "I know I will never see a better example of pure raw leadership."

My later life hero Edward A. "Ned" Shuman, III's graduation picture, class of 1954. (Courtesy of the U.S. Naval Academy Special Collections and Archives)

An accomplished pilot—a Navy test pilot, in fact—Ned Shuman flew 17 combat missions over Vietnam before he was forced to eject from his plane, breaking his arm and shoulder, and was taken prisoner. Ned spent the first 17 months in solitary confinement, losing 50 pounds, and being beaten often with a rubber whip. Eventually, he was put with other U.S. prisoners at the infamous compound dubbed the "Hanoi Hilton." At one point, their Vietnamese captors removed a group of 43 U.S. servicemen from their cells into a single holding area. The first Sunday they were together they attempted to hold a church service but were threatened with severe punishment. The following week, Ned, as the most senior officer in the group, asked each prisoner if he wanted to hold a church service in the face of threats. After obtaining agreement from the other 42 men, the following Sunday, Ned began leading the group in the Lord's Prayer. The guards grabbed him and took him away to be tortured. Then the second ranking officer stood up and started the prayer, and the guards hauled him off for beating. Then the number three officer stood up; then number four; then number five. Finally, the frustrated guards gave up, and the remaining POWs finished the Lord's Prayer.

Sitting in Regina's one day having sandwiches, I asked Ned about the Lord's Prayer incident. His immediate reaction was typical Ned. "When you're the senior officer, it ain't good," he quipped. "Before the prayer," he explained," I put on all the extra clothes I had because I knew what was coming. They beat me, put me in solitary with my legs in stocks, and I stayed there for six weeks." Such courage is astonishing to me, whose greatest physical punishment was a hand on the rear as a child.

Released from the North Vietnam prison in 1973, Ned was hospitalized to recover from his injuries, then resumed a successful Navy career commanding several Naval Air Stations before his retirement in 1984. One thing Ned never talked about was his medals, but if you saw pictures of him in uniform, he had a chest full of them, including one of the nation's highest military honors, the Silver Star. Ned's Silver Star citation reads:

> For conspicuous gallantry and intrepidity while interned as a prisoner of War in North Vietnam. In September 1969, his captors, completely ignoring international agreements, subjected him to extreme mental and physical cruelties in an attempt to obtain military information and false confessions for propaganda purposes. Through his resistance to those brutalities, he contributed significantly toward the eventual abandonment of harsh treatment by the North Vietnamese, which was attracting international attention. By his determination, courage, resourcefulness, and devotion to duty, he reflected great credit upon himself and upheld the highest traditions of the Naval Service and the United States Armed Forces.

Despite his POW ordeal, Ned seemed to enjoy his retirement. He claimed that he barely thought about being a prisoner of war. He had his plane, which he still flew into his 80s, his poker games, and his sailboat. The boat finally did what the Viet Cong couldn't. On his way to a goose hunt in 2013, Ned fell in the boat and ultimately passed away from ensuing complications. I miss his craggy laugh.

Being an Annapolitan, it's hard not being a Navy fan, and I've been one all my life. The only time I root against Navy teams is when they play my alma mater, The University of Maryland. But there is something inspiring and sentimental that fills me with joy whenever I hear it, and it's not my college song. It is the Academy's alma mater, which has thrilled me since childhood when sung by the brigade after every football game. Today, still, after every televised Army-Navy game I leave the TV on to hear the mids, with the football team gathered together on the field in front of the brigade, sing *Navy Blue and Gold*:

> *Now college men from sea to sea may sing of colors true,*
> *But who has better right than we, to hoist a symbol hue?*
> *For sailor men in battle fair, since fighting days of old,*
> *Have proved the sailor's right to wear, the Navy Blue and Gold!*
> *Beat Army!*

CHAPTER FOURTEEN

GROWING UP—FROM DEPRESSION BABY TO WARTIME YOUTH

My dad's job at the Naval Academy was a blessing in many ways, none more important than in days of his marriage to my mother on St. Patrick's Day, 1932, and my birth in 1933. It was the time of the Great Depression, and a job at the Academy meant a steady pay day for us when many others struggled or were jobless.

Nineteen thirty three was a monumental year in the United States—certainly not because of my birth—but because of the watershed events that impacted the U.S. and all of its Main Streets. Franklin Delano Roosevelt took office as President on March 4, 1933 and immediately instituted his economic plans, called the New Deal, that helped abate the depression. Besides passing New Deal legislation, Congress made some momentous decisions. It recognized the independence of the Philippines, passed the first minimum wage law (33 cents per hour) and, just weeks before Roosevelt's inauguration, Congress repealed the failed experiment of Prohibition, which had banned alcohol in the U.S.

Even the face of the country began to change, including the start of construction of such landmarks as the Golden Gate Bridge; dedication of Mount Rushmore, and nationwide viewing of the two-year-old Empire State Building in the film *King Kong*. On the journalism front, 1933 saw the publication of the first issues of *Newsweek* and *Esquire*. On the lighter side, in 1933 the *Lone Ranger* was born as a radio hero; the game of Monopoly was invented; they played the first major league all-star baseball game; and Walt Disney released his iconic movie *Three Little Pigs*.

In January, in a prelude to violence and evil, Nazi leader Adolf Hitler was appointed German Chancellor and his reign of terror began with the completion of Dachau, the first Nazi concentration camp. Soon after, an act was passed making Hitler dictator of Germany, and he formed the Gestapo secret police. Thus, the seeds of World War II were planted.

In 1933, more than 12 million Americans remained unemployed, some 30% of the working age population, and Americans overall had about half as much income as in 1929, before the stock market crash. Also by 1933, the value of stock on the New York Stock Exchange was less than a fifth of what it had been at its 1929 peak. While the depression left deep scars on my parents' generation, those scars were not so deep on most Annapolitans. The reasons: we had the Naval Academy and the Chesapeake Bay. The Academy, with its sister facility, The Engineering Experiment Station at North Severn, supplied government jobs for workers like my father. But even the Academy was not immune to the depression. In 1933, a federal budget cut forced the Academy to lay off 20 professors and instructors and 90 laborers and building attendants. Luckily for us, my dad survived the layoff. Even though he made about $1,000 a year, when the average salary was $1,500, my mother's frugality (and sporadic jobs) allowed us to live comfortably. The Bay not only let watermen earn sustaining dollars, it supplied food for those having trouble making ends meet. Most of the year, you could catch your meal of fish, crabs or oysters. It was better than the out-of-work Kentucky miners who tried to live on dandelions. Many of those local Annapolis folks ate so much seafood, they couldn't bear to consume it later in life.

My mother saved money in depression days and in the 40s by recycling clothes, darning holey socks, turning the frayed collars on our shirts and patching worn sweater elbows and trouser knees. I recall her even cutting down a pair of my long pants with ragged cuffs to make shorts.

I believe the depression had something to do with my being an only child. Mom always claimed it was because she had a difficult pregnancy and delivery with me, but I think the fear of having another mouth to feed played an equal if not greater part in that decision. In fact, birth rates during the depression fell to their lowest point in the nation's history. My generation of children born in the 1930s would be the smallest of the 20th century.

A Mismatched Pair

Being an only child, for me, was fortuitous. The cost of braces for my buck teeth and college were difficult enough financially. With a brother or sister or two, I'd have probably grown up looking like Bugs Bunny, and who knows what social stigma that would have caused. Speaking of stigmas growing up, I carried one with me from my parents' interreligious marriage. I have often wondered what caused my parents to marry. Certainly there was a physical attraction and some social forces that brought them together, but their differences were enormous.

When dad was in his late 20s, he lived with some friends on a houseboat moored somewhere around the City Dock. He never told me any details of living on that boat, but whenever he mentioned it, he would get a twinkle in his eyes in remembrance of some past escapades. It was with those boat-living buddies that dad would travel to Baltimore and its more urbane dance halls, mostly speakeasies where they could avoid prohibition.

It was at a dance in Baltimore that he met the 19-year-old Lillian Wolf and fell in love with this raven-haired young lady who would become his wife, my mother. My dad was a good-looking "older" man of 30; my mother, tall and fair-skinned with a voluptuous figure. The physical attraction seems apparent.

Yet, if there were two people more unsuited, I can't think of them. Dad was a small-town guy, a Methodist, and somewhat bigoted when it came to religion and skin color. My mother was Jewish and from a strict family with 10 brothers watching over her. I'm sure her desire to escape the rigid, conservative household played a part in her willingness to elope with my father. But elope she did to be married by a Methodist preacher in Annapolis. An Italian friend of my father was best man, and mom would joke about their ecumenical service: "A Jew marrying a Methodist with a Catholic standing for them, shook up Annapolis," she said.

My dad was a mild-mannered man who seldom lost his temper. There were stories of wild escapades as a young man who wasn't afraid of anyone, but I only saw the fearsome side of him once. At age eight or nine I sassed him over and over until his anger reached the boiling point, and he hit me hard, knocking me to the floor. He was so upset with what he had done that he never hit me again— not even a simple spanking when I deserved it, which was often.

Discipline was left to my mother and an occasional slap or spanking was doled out when in order, but her greatest punishment weapon were those awful words, "Get in your room. You can't go out and play!" I dreaded those words more than a few licks of her hand. There never was a belt or rod raised in anger in our home.

While my dad didn't spank me, he also didn't hug me much. Like many men of his generation, outward displays of affection were rare. Perhaps on a happy Christmas morning when a gift excited me, he'd allow for a hug and a kiss on the cheek. It wasn't until I was an adult that a hug and a kiss on the cheek were more readily accepted by my father.

My mom, on the other hand, would not let me leave the apartment without a "kiss me goodbye" refrain. Mom was needy that way, and while I enjoyed our loving embraces, it fostered an obligation towards her that would never leave. Even as an adult, if I didn't call her for a few days, I could feel her unstated disapproval when we finally talked, so I seldom let much time go by between calls or visits. Dad couldn't have cared less.

What a mismatched pair, my mom and dad. My parents had their differences, but they stayed together until death did them part.

Being from a mixed marriage in the '30s and '40s was no joke. It was a burden in my youth, and I'll detail how in the later chapter on "Tolerance vs. Intolerance." My mother's family disowned her when she ran off with my father, but my birth softened them and mom reunited with them when I was a baby. The Baltimore kin not only eventually accepted my dad, but they embraced this likeable gentile from Annapolis. The one benefit for me as a child was to get Christmas presents in Annapolis and Hanukkah money in Baltimore during the holidays.

Making Money

Money, it seems, was always on our minds. From the time I was 10, I don't believe there was a time when I didn't have a job, especially in the summer. Mostly it was grocery store work, from the days in the Maggio's produce store, to Mr. Brady's small grocery on the corner of Conduit and Union Streets, to the Acme on West Street, a chain store, and finally to the Community Market downtown when I needed money for college.

Though the job at the Community Market on Dock Street was menial—stocking groceries, sweeping the floor and the much-hated chore of cleaning the bloody meat trays—work itself never bothered me. Whether it was selling crabs, cleaning up at Maggio's, or jerking sodas at the Hitching Post, being an usher at the Republic Theater, building my own snowball stand, hauling ice to boats at the Annapolis Yacht basin, or selling and delivering papers, it was the quest for money that motivated this Main Street boy. Yet, I didn't keep the money. I always gave it to my mother, who would allot me a small amount of spending money, using the rest mainly to buy me clothes or for family entertainment. The one good thing about helping to earn your way at an early age—it produced a work ethic that remained through life.

Probably the best job I had was soda-jerking at the Hitching Post, a small restaurant on Prince Georges Street near Maryland Avenue heavily frequented by midshipmen. The restaurant got its name from the black, metal post topped by a miniature horse's head with a ring through its nose that stood out front mimicking the colonial era post for tethering a horse. The restaurant is long gone, but the hitching post remains. I call it the best job because of the free ice cream and cokes we soda jerks consumed and the juke box that continually serenaded us with such popular songs as Frankie Lane's "Mule Train," Vaughn Monroe's "Ghost Riders in the Sky," The Andrews Sisters' "I Can Dream Can't I?," and Bing Crosby's "Deep in the Heart of Texas."

The worst job I ever had, as mentioned earlier, was working with my dad spreading hot black tar on the roof in sun-baking, 90 degree heat. That experience confirmed for me to follow my mother's inclination, not my father's, and get a college education.

My education began at the Green Street school, officially known as Annapolis Elementary. I entered grammar school in 1940 the beginning of a decade that would change the world. It was a decade of wars—World War II, the Korean War and the Cold War.

Green Street school was built on the site of the town house of Dr. Charles Carroll, who also built the grand house on the corner of Main and Conduit Streets, where his son Charles Carroll the Barrister would be born. The stone wall along the sidewalk in front of the school, a climbing and walking wall for me and my grammar school buddies, probably dates from Dr. Carroll's time—and it's still there.

WWII

My grammar school buddies were an eclectic lot, and though we produced no Einsteins or Joe DiMaggios, many of them succeeded in life, by the standard measure, becoming educators, doctors, lawyers, politicians, judges and journalists. Some did less well, spending their days in menial jobs or fighting alcoholism. The same can be said of most grammar school classes, I'm sure. But, in one way, we were different. In December of our second grade year, the Japanese bombed Pearl Harbor.

My mother and I were in Baltimore visiting my aunt on Sunday, December 7, 1941, and I was playing with my cousin, Ralph Carp, (also named after our maternal grandfather), when the radio broadcast the news of the Japanese attack. The next day, President Roosevelt made his famous "a date which will live in infamy" speech to Congress, which declared war against Japan. At almost eight years old, the impact of those words was lost on me. But the events that followed would change the world we lived in, including my small world in Annapolis, which was a microcosm of America at war.

Young men, such as my Uncle Burgan Crosby, the baby of the family, were drafted at 18, the youngest age for compulsory service. Although men up to age 64 had to register for the draft, only those under 38 normally were called. My dad was 40. While many men volunteered, nearly ten million were drafted. I watched my Uncle Burgan go off to war, amid my grandmother's tears, and I had no idea of the dangers he would face in the Army's battles on what was called "The Road to Rome."

My Uncle Burgan Crosby, my father's youngest sibling, shown here during World War II, when he served in Italy.

The "Road to Rome" was actually documented in a small pamphlet featuring black silhouettes of rifle-carrying soldiers moving under three flags—the U.S., Great Britain and France—with the "A5" uniform of the Fifth Army alongside the flags. This booklet was given to the soldiers who made that march.

The booklet outlines the awful battle for Rome that started out in Salerno and went through the killing fields of Naples, Volturno,

Cassino and Anzio. The forward to the pamphlet by the Campaign's Commander, Lieutenant General Mark Clark, speaks to the soldiers who fought their way through these hellish battles. He wrote:

To the Officers and Men of the Fifth Army:

> *You have been privileged to make history. You have taken the "Eternal City." You have done what the forces of the famous Carthaginian, Hannibal, failed to do. You captured Rome from the south.*
>
> *You are liberators, not conquerors. You came to this sacred spot to drive out the enemy. You did so gallantly and effectively. All Rome welcomed you.*
>
> *This is your book. It relates briefly the story of our great struggle from the time of our arrival in Italy until we entered Rome, and it tells you something about the action of different units.*
>
> *Those of our comrades who gave their lives did not do so in vain. Their spirits are with us as we continue the campaign in which they played so glorious a part.*
>
> *Your country is proud of you. The Allied cause has profited by your military deeds. Italy, which has known soldiers of many races, of many nations, of many armies, will not forget you. You have a place in the ageless record of a city around which ancient and medieval civilizations flourished.*

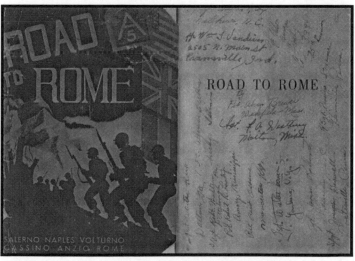

My Uncle Burgan's copy of "Road to Rome," a small pamphlet given to Fifth Army soldiers who fought their way from Salerno to Rome. His copy was signed by several of his company's soldiers from all over the U.S.

Although the booklet is a panegyric—an elaborate, noncritical praise of the Fifth Army's assault in Italy—it is instructive about what war was like in the middle of the 20th century and what a young soldier, such as my Uncle Burgan, experienced in World War II. Burgan gave the booklet to my cousin Albert, who passed it on to me. To read the much thumbed booklet was made even more personal because Burgan had it signed, much like a school yearbook, by some of his company E, 339th Regiment, 85th Division mates. They were representative of the U.S.—Sergeants and Privates from such towns as Matthews, N.C.; Evansville, Ind.; Morton, Miss.; Dalton, Ga.; Chicago, Ill.; Manchester, Ky.; Yonkers, N.Y.; Laurens, S.C.; and Coatesville, Pa.

The facts of the taking of Rome don't quite jibe with the booklet, given that General Clark was later criticized for failure to exploit his position in a quest to liberate Rome, allowing a substantial number of German units to escape to reinforce other units in Italy.

However, that mattered little to my Uncle Burgan and his fellow soldiers. Liberating Rome was a respite after nine months of fighting and thousands of casualties.

Like many of his "greatest generation," Burgan talked little about the war. When I once asked him what is war like to actually fight, he responded that he wouldn't know because he "was too busy finding something to hide behind."

He did tell my cousin Albert about an experience reminiscent of the scene in the movie "Saving Private Ryan," in which the American soldiers enter a house where German soldiers are hiding. Unlike the movie, no one was killed because as Burgan's team went upstairs, the German soldiers apparently left from the basement. Whether they engaged the Germans, Albert didn't know.

A number of local Annapolis area men were killed in World War II, including two brothers and a cousin from one family. How that family should suffer such bad luck is tragic.

Burgan returned from the war, put his campaign medals and autographed booklet away and resumed his ordinary life, working at the Naval Academy as a paymaster, with lots of dating and dancing but never a marriage. He lived for many years in that third floor Main Street apartment where his parents had lived. He would join my family for an occasional holiday meal, but he mostly kept to himself or met with a few old friends. Burgan died in 2004 at the age of 81 and was buried with full military honors, including the mournful bugle sounds of "Taps," which he well deserved for those frightful years on the road to Rome.

My mother's youngest brother, Jerry, was also an infantryman during the war. His division originally was sent to protect the Panama Canal Zone, where he contracted a rare skin condition and was sent home to recover. Thus he was stateside when his unit went to the Pacific war zone, where it took heavy casualties.

Very few American families with young sons escaped the traumas of World War II. Though my uncles, Burgan and Jerry, escaped serious injury, they were forever changed by their war experiences.

When the war started, my mom thought my dad ought to join the Seabees, the Navy's construction team. She didn't realize the Seabees were not behind the lines builders, but front line path makers whose death and wounding rate was among the Navy's highest. Instead, my dad ended up as an air raid warden, walking the downtown streets at night making sure anyone with lights on had their black shades drawn so enemy planes had no easy target. Thinking the enemy would bomb Annapolis is laughable now, but the fear was real then and, in fact, German submariners used backlighting of East Coast cities to destroy ships exiting harbors. The black shades were pulled down on our front room windows as we listened to war news on the radio from the likes of Walter Winchell, with his sensationalist, staccato delivery of battle news mixed with celebrity gossip. The radio was our connection to the world outside of Annapolis. The only time we got close to the enemy was at the city dock, when a shiny, black, captured Japanese midget submarine was on display as part of a war bond drive. The sub, HA. 10, was part of the Japanese attack on Pearl Harbor, but ran aground and was captured before it could do any damage. Both we kids and our parents lined up to view the sub, as if it was a holiday treat rather than a vestige of Japanese infamy.

At school the bomb threat was considered a serious matter. We were taught to hide under our desks when the air raid siren sounded, and we practiced it often. As young as we were, we felt the impact of the war in many ways. Rationing of sugar, meat, coffee and other food stuffs led to eating more leftovers and planting "victory gardens," such as the one I tried to plant in the little strip of dirt behind our apartment house. It didn't grow. I remember collecting the metal foil coating paper in cigarette packs and searching for scrap metal in back yards, basements and empty lots for scrap drives. Along with my Boy Scout Troop, number 335, I earned the "General Eisenhower War Service Medal for Extraordinary Patriots Achievement" by collecting more than one thousand pounds of waste paper for the war effort during March-April 1945. I remember kneading the little red dot of dye in the white margarine package to make it look more like butter. I recall pasting ten cent war bond stamps in a booklet that, when filled up with 187 stamps, would be traded for a full-fledged War Bond. My dad bought one out of his pay every month. Those bonds, costing $18.75 and worth $25 in ten years, helped finance the war effort. We kids actually felt our small actions were helping win the war, and we took pride in that. Of course, adults on the home front had to deal with even more shortages—of housing, gasoline, nylon, rubber, etc. My family had three books of rationing stamps that had to be presented when purchasing the rationed items, in quantities such as one pound of butter, coffee or sugar, so my mom guarded the books carefully. Whenever someone complained, the common response was, "Don't you know there's a war going on?"

While we youngsters felt the impact of shortages, we were somewhat insulated from the horrors of war. Unless you were like my dear friend and classmate Meta Holmes, whose Naval Officer father was killed in the war (memorialized by the Gold Star in the window), the only place we really felt the terror of battle and hatred of the enemy was at the movies. During the war, for 10 cents at the Republic Theater next door or the Circle Theater on State Circle, we would watch Humphrey Bogart take us into *Action in The North Atlantic* against the Germans or *Across the Pacific* to fight the Japanese. Spencer Tracy flew us for *Thirty Seconds Over Tokyo*, and John Wayne was a *Flying Tiger*, one of the *Fighting Seabees*, or took us *Back to Bataan*. Personally, I preferred the *Dumbo* and *Bambi* films, but the war movies surely made us hate the "Japs" and "Nazis," and it took years to shake off the hatred built in youth. Just think, a 1944 opinion poll found that 13% of the U.S. public favored killing all Japanese. Though Annapolis has felt deeply the impact of every U.S. war—and the Naval Academy has monuments galore to prove it—the only battle fought on its soil or sea was one of the first ever in the colonies—the Battle of the Severn.

My favorite summer swimming haunt, Horn Point—site of such historic events as President Washington aground on a sandbar, Lafayette marching his troops, a Revolutionary War fort, and a Civil War hospital—also appears to have been the scene of this early religious war.

The settlers who founded Providence grew quickly in numbers, soon outnumbering the Catholics, and when Proprietor Cecil Calvert's governor, William Stone, insisted that all citizens take an oath of fidelity to the Catholic Proprietor, the Puritans protested.

In retaliation, Stone commissioned and armed a group of Calvert's supporters to plan an attack on Providence, but the Puritans learned of the plot and prepared for battle, which took place on March 25, 1655. While contemporary accounts do not describe the exact location of the battle, many historians believe it was fought at the mouth of the Severn, ending on what was Horn Point, where Puritan forces quickly drove Stone's Catholic fighters to the water's edge. The battle was over in less than half an hour. Nineteen men died in the battle and four Catholic prisoners were executed. While the Puritans recognized Lord Baltimore/Cecil Calvert's proprietorship, they now dominated Maryland despite the proprietor's religion.

Growing up during World War II and the Korean War and, as an adult hearing of the ravage of the Vietnam War, Iraq, Afghanistan, and wars everywhere, has made me realize, reluctantly, that war is in the heart of man. As Plato wrote, "Only the dead have seen the end of war."

As the Second World War wound down in 1945, when I was in fifth grade, on April 12, the radio sent a shocking message across America. Franklin Roosevelt was dead. The man who had led the country out of depression and through the Second World War would not live to see the war end. The grief was palpable. Among the working class folks in our circle, almost all Democrats, it was as if they had lost a very close relative. After all, he had been our political father for almost twelve years. I remember my mother sobbing at the news, and our teachers were somber on our return to school and, as later movie newsreels showed us, the grief spread throughout America.

HAPPY SCHOOL DAYS
1946-1947

As my grammar school days ended, the era of War was over, only to be replaced by another era of fear, the atomic age.

Then, on the same movie screens, in August of 1945, the newsreels showed the giant mushroom clouds of the atomic bombs dropped on Hiroshima and Nagasaki in Japan. We were happy to hear that these devastating bombs would end the war, but we didn't realize they would also usher in a new era of fear.

CHAPTER FIFTEEN

"DUCK AND COVER" HIGH SCHOOL DAYS

In the new, 1950s nuclear age, the fear of war came back to us in high school, and we found ourselves once again reacting to air raid drills, sitting on the school's bottom floor hallways with no windows until the "all clear" sounded. We were told to put our hands over our heads for protection. They called it "duck and cover." What protection against nuclear attack they expected of that move I didn't understand, though a smaller, lower target would present some protection from radiation and flying debris if the blast was some distance away. A more sensible suggestion from the government was to build in-home or outside fallout shelters, and some did.

All of this fearful activity was brought about by the dual threats of Russia and communism. By the time I was a freshman in high school, Soviet-influenced communism became the bogeyman of America. We suffered through the fear-mongering era of Joseph McCarthy's Un-American Activities Committee, U.S. intervention in Korea in 1950 to keep communists from taking over the country, and the "Cold War," which fostered an era of suspicion and black-listing. Talk about "un-American!"

By the beginning of my junior year in high school, September 1950, we were hearing about this great crusader, Senator Joseph McCarthy, a Wisconsin Republican, who was rooting out communists from our major institutions—government, the arts, even the military. In a speech to a Republican Women's Club of Wheeling, West Virginia, he waved a list he claimed had 205 names of known communists working for the U.S. State Department. His claim was published by a local paper and then spread across the major media of the country. Thus, "McCarthyism" was born. Anti-communist fever in the early 1950s, some of it abetted by conservative politicians who equated President Roosevelt's New Deal with communism, was commandeered by Senator McCarthy. But the term "McCarthyism" became a dirty word, meaning to make false or misleading accusations without real proof. No one ever saw the 205 names on McCarthy's list. McCarthy was a

phony—and an alcoholic to boot. By the time he was unmasked
and censured by his fellow senators in 1954 for "conduct that tends
to bring the Senate into dishonor and disrepute," some of our
greatest writers and actors were blacklisted, thus deprived of their
livelihood, hundreds of citizens were imprisoned and more than ten
thousand lost their jobs. As David Halberstam writes of McCarthy,
in his book, *The Fifties*: "In the end he produced little beyond fear
and headlines. After a thousand speeches and a thousand charges,
the last thing in the world he could probably have recognized was
a real communist or a real spy ring." In 1954, my college mates
and I actually witnessed McCarthy's decline on television in what
was known as the "Army-McCarthy hearings." His accusations
of communists in the Army led to live television coverage, which
showed McCarthy to be a bullying, blustering fraud, and his
popularity nose-dived among us college kids and Americans in
general. Three years later, a victim of his drinking, McCarthy was
dead. As David Halberstam summed up the McCarthy era:

> McCarthy's carnival-like four-year spree of accusations,
> charges, and threats touched something deep in the
> American body politic, something that lasted long after
> his own recklessness, carelessness, and boozing ended
> his career in shame. McCarthyism crystallized and
> politicized the anxieties of a nation living in a dangerous
> new era. He took people who were at the worst guilty of
> political naïveté and accused them of treason. He set out
> to do the unthinkable, and it turned out to be surprisingly
> thinkable.

While we teens in high school felt the peripheral impact of the
Cold War threats, by and large those were carefree years. In my
family's household, the 1950s brought our first telephone, albeit a
party line shared by several families, and our first television set,
a 12-inch black and white with a rabbit ears antenna and a fuzzy
picture, good enough to watch "I Love Lucy," or my favorite
Saturday morning cartoons or western movies. Annapolis, like
most of America, responded happily to post-war abundance,
buying TVs and cars and other goods and luxuries unavailable in
preceding years. Some called it "the fabulous fifties."

This experience was explained succinctly by Eugenia Kaledin,
in her study "Daily Life in the United States 1940-1959—Shifting
Worlds." She wrote:

Perhaps the mass production and efficiency Americans have always admired inspired many to think of the '50s as 'fabulous.' Coming after the poverty of the 1930s and the austerity of the 1940s, the pursuit of happiness—as it found expression in the great range of material goods in the 1950s—made many forget the Cold War. Not just hula hoops, Davy Crockett hats, deodorants and chlorophyll toothpaste, and Elvis Presley and Marilyn Monroe—the popular culture symbols of the time—but a world that seemed to cater to every possible taste emerged to satisfy a great variety of needs.

My high school years were full of friendships and memories that have lasted a lifetime. It all started with walking to school. Annapolis High School, a large red brick building, foreboding at first but ultimately friendly, was just about one mile from 183 Main Street, and depending on what route I took—down Conduit Street and through the residential neighborhoods or up Main and out West Street—I would hook up with any number of classmates. Walking to high school with buddies was the best part of the day. If I was with John Henneberger, we might stop at the Little Tavern on West Street for a ten cent hamburger for breakfast. If we walked the neighborhood route, we might stop at Warren Klawans' home on Southgate Avenue so Warren could drive us the last half mile to school, allowing us to show off as we whizzed past our classmates.

A Smoking Story

For those of us who smoked, we'd stop at the fire hydrant on the street before reaching school property. The hydrant was the demarcation point for smoking. Smoking past that was subject to school discipline. Smoking in school, such as stealing a few puffs in the bathroom, as we did on several occasions, could mean expulsion. We didn't know it then, but we were addicted, as were many of our parents. My mom and dad both smoked, so it seemed natural to me. (Like so many smokers, they both eventually would develop cancer.) When they found out I had started smoking at 15, my parents' only admonishment was, "You can't smoke on Main Street until you're sixteen."

The government didn't start closing in on cigarette companies until the mid-1950s, when the Surgeon General first publicly linked smoking to lung cancer. Even then, it was fashionable to smoke, egged on by movies and television, where the stars often had a cigarette in hand or mouth, or tobacco company ads promising health and popularity.

Funny thing: it was an ad that finally convinced me to quit smoking in my mid-30s. In fact, as a Washington journalist in 1964, I witnessed a report by the Surgeon General's office on cigarette's damage to health, replete with photos of cancerous lungs. I got so upset, I went out in the hall to have a smoke to calm my nerves. That's how ingrained the habit was. In the next few years I made several attempts at trying to quit and failing before I saw the ad that forced me to quit.

Back in 1967, when my son, Raymond, was five years old and I was a 2-pack-a-day cigarette smoker, I happened to see a TV commercial from the American Heart Association titled "Like Father, Like Son." It depicted a father doing chores that his young four- or five-year-old copied. Then, they sit down at a tree together, the dad lights up a cigarette and drops the pack at his side, where the son is sitting. The little boy picks up the pack and starts to take out a cigarette. The announcer's final words were, "Like Father, Like Son—Think about it." I thought about it and quit on the spot. Not that quitting was easy, but I never smoked again, and it gave me the ammunition later to stop my then teenage son from smoking—without my being a hypocrite. For me, all the statistics about the evils of smoking, including the Surgeon General's report on smoking's disastrous results, were nowhere near as powerful as that one story about father and son. I'm thankful for that because the power of the cigarette habit consumes the smoker. I kept my pack of cigarettes in my shirt pocket, and in busy times, I'd automatically reach for one. In fact, when I became a journalist writing copy, especially on deadline, I'd get so engrossed I'd have a couple cigarettes lit in the ashtray at the same time. The habit was so strong that in stressful situations, at least a year after I quit smoking, I'd find myself automatically reaching in my shirt pocket for that nonexistent cigarette.

Unusual Teachers

In high school I began to hone my writing skills, with sports stories for our school newspaper, the *Tally-Ho*; through my supportive junior year English teacher, Miss Elizabeth Davis, who let me write a short fiction piece instead of a book report and gave me an "A" for the rather juvenile story about a drug addict; and through the questioning of my writing skills by my senior year English teacher, Miss Mary Katherine Cox. On a class assignment from Miss Cox to write a poem, I submitted one about the years of growing as a high schooler, called "Four Years." When I read it to the class, Miss Cox, with her usual tight-lipped stare beneath graying hair, asked me accusingly if I had copied it from somewhere. What a back-handed compliment! However, the poem was a hit and was read at an assembly of the entire student body and was printed in the *Tally-Ho*, a great boost for the ego of the writer within me.

Miss Cox was probably the most dreaded of Annapolis High School teachers. She was a no nonsense teacher who lacked mirth and demanded excellence. We feared her, but we worked hard to please her. She used the *Reader's Digest* word quiz to drill us and made us memorize a long list of words and their meanings. My mother had an answer for these memorizations, a creative word game. One example I will never forget was the word "trauma." I memorized the definition through a sentence we made up: *"Throw ma out the window and she will get a condition resulting from shock or injury."* I aced Miss Cox's word tests, and as Miss Cox undoubtedly planned, greatly expanded my vocabulary.

While Miss Cox was our most demanding high school teacher, the most unusual teacher I ever had, high school or college, was Anthony Bischoff, who taught science at Annapolis High, and was my Junior year home room teacher. A round-faced, balding man, with a rough-hewn look and hair growing out of his ears, I believe he was an example of peculiar genius. When he was thinking by the blackboard, he'd stick a piece of chalk in his ear. If he spotted an inattentive student, he'd throw the chalk at that miscreant or even toss an eraser. He'd usually miss, perhaps on purpose. His most unusual trait, however, was his unique talent for calling us by our names spelled backward. He called John Henneberger "Mr. Regrebenneh;" Warren Klawans was "Mr. Snawalk, and I was "Mr. Ybsorc, pronounced "Ibsorc."

Writing for the *Tally-Ho* helped cement my passion for journalism, but it was more about friendships than writing. Fellow Tally-Ho reporters included my friend, Gregg Magruder. I spent considerable time at Gregg's house on Revell Street, which goes down to Spa Creek from Shipwright Street, starting about where the Upton Scott house sits. Whatever time we spent indoors was accompanied by Gregg's collection of 45 RPM records of Nat King Cole's hit songs—"Mona Lisa," "Nature Boy," Too Young," "Unforgettable," etc. My friend Warren Klawans was a photographer on that *Tally-Ho* staff, as was a younger camera guy, Stanley Stearns, who I would later bump into in Washington, D.C., both of us in Journalism, and where he would take the iconic photo of a three-year-old John F. Kennedy, Jr. saluting the coffin of his assassinated father, the President.

My favorite high school teacher was Miss Davis, a kind, soft spoken lady, with a pretty face beneath wavy, dark hair, always ready with a smile, a bit stylish wearing her necklace of pearls, sort of an anti-Miss Cox. She was also my most influential teacher. Not only did she expose us to classic literature, but acting like a latter day librarian Esther King, suggested I might enjoy some other writers. She mentioned nothing revolutionary, just the new classics from the 30s—Hemingway, Fitzgerald and Steinbeck. Those reading explorations led to my reading Erskine Caldwell's novel *Tobacco Road*, which introduced me to both the impoverished and sexual lives of rural southerners. Then, on the lookout for literature for my generation, I heard the drum beat for a new novel and novelist, J.D. Salinger and his *The Catcher in the Rye*. Although as a senior in high school I didn't relate to the adolescent alienation of his protagonist Holden Caulfield, I began to feel the rebellion bubbling up around us.

The sense of alienation and rebellion in the early 1950s was stimulated by Salinger's writings, a prelude to Jack Kerouac and the beat writers, along with the much criticized gyrations of singer Elvis Presley, the depiction of *The Wild One* in movies starring Marlon Brando, and the embodiment of *Rebel Without A Cause*, in movies and real life, by actor James Dean.

The question arises: were the early 1950s fearful, rebellious or fantastic? For those fighting in Korea or on the front lines of the nascent civil rights movement, the times were fearful; for a purveyor of alienation such as Salinger, they were rebellious times; and for me and my high school mates, the era was fabulous. High school was a blast, and many of us would continue those fun times in college.

Transition to College

I wasn't the first in my family to attend college. My mother's youngest brother, Jerry, graduated from The University of Baltimore. My father's brother Douglas, fourth oldest among his siblings, went to Western Maryland College, where he was a champion boxer. My dad often told the story of Douglas' return to town to box against the Navy team. Half the men in Annapolis turned out to watch, dad exaggerated, only to see Annapolis' own Doug Crosby get knocked out.

My dad would not have minded if I, too, was a sheet metal worker, but thankfully, my mother saw me with a college education. That wasn't as easy as it might sound today. Since paying for college didn't seem to be in the cards on my father's salary, a free education at the Naval Academy appeared the best bet. In fact, I joined the Naval Reserve while in high school so I could more easily seek an appointment to the Academy. My high school senior yearbook lists me as "a future midshipman in the U.S.N.A." In 1952, seniors at my high school were given an eye test, and much to my surprise, they discovered I was near-sighted. This was no great tragedy, but it upset my plans for a free college education at the Naval Academy, where 20-20 vision was an entrance requirement. To check this out, my dad took me to the Navy doctor who gave the entry eye exams. I failed, and so ended my naval career, thank the Lord. I'm not sure I could have handled the military and academic discipline of the Academy. Also, I was more inclined to the humanities than the sciences, and at the Academy in those days science and math were front and center.

So, it was fortuitous when my failed eye exam shattered those plans. You don't study journalism at the Naval Academy.

Once again, mom to the rescue. She took a job as a secretary at a local insurance company and, with my job at the Community Market, the three of us put together the tuition and room and board costs for The University of Maryland. In the current days of multi-thousand dollar tuition (Maryland is close to $20,000 for in-state students) it's hard to believe it cost only $476 for tuition and low-end housing in 1952, which probably doubled with food and books. But we stretched to get that unlordly sum. I even lived in wooden, temporary housing units built for returning World War II veterans, because they cost $50 per semester as opposed to $70 for a regular dorm room. And I jerked sodas in the University's dairy bar to supplement our finances, and when I was on the lacrosse team, I got free dinners in the University dining hall.

The task of handling the transition from high school to college was formidable, but the transition from insular Annapolitan life to a huge college campus, with its greater sophistication and more cosmopolitan social life, was transformational. An allowable beer drinking age of 18 took me to the jazz clubs of nearby Washington, D.C. Journalism classes took me to the city desk of the *Baltimore*

Sun, the National Press Club in D.C., and *Reader's Digest* offices in New York with a stay in New York City. Main Street looks a bit different after you've spent some time in Greenwich Village.

My experience in New York City with my senior journalism class in 1956 was quite educational, and I don't mean academically. A few of us spent one evening at the Village Vanguard in Greenwich Village listening to a marvelous young black singer with unbelievable range. His name: Johnny Mathis. We were quite surprised when, between acts, he would sit at a table with the best looking, young, white girl in the place. At that time, few of us had seen interracial dating. But it was his voice that enchanted us more than his girlfriend surprised us. Several years later, Johnny Mathis was a big hit and, when he came to Baltimore for a concert, I interviewed him at the *News-Post* offices. I recall asking him how he managed such range with his voice. His response, as I recall it, "I don't think about it; I just sing it." He sang it wonderfully for the next 50 years.

The next night in New York, we were invited to a party at the home of a classmate's friend or relative. I spent the evening talking to some attractive, seemingly sophisticated, 30-something young ladies. When my classmates pulled me away from all that attention, saying we had to get back to our hotel, two of the young ladies begged me to stay. I could even sleep in the apartment, they suggested. I declined and went off with my friends. It wasn't until later that I realized those young ladies might have had more on their minds than talking. If so, I was too naïve to see it.

At about the same time as the Reader's Digest trip, I entered a novella I had written in a new writers contest put on by a respected New York publisher. The story, titled "The Best," centered around a small town pool shark. Of course, the story grew out of my experiences shooting pool in "Pap's." While I didn't win the contest, I received a personal—not a form—letter suggesting that my novella showed promise, and the publisher would be glad to look at any of my future work.

The New York trip and the publisher's letter got me thinking about moving to New York and trying my luck as a writer. But those thoughts evaporated in the culture of my generation, where knowledge of financial troubles of the Great Depression and fear caused by World War II made us more oriented toward a good job, a home and family. I decided that course was best for me. Of course, a young lady named Carlotta had a lot to do with my decision. For me, too, there was that sense of obligation to my parents, to be around for them as they had always been for me.

My wife, Carlotta, and I at the Boston Commons on our New England
honeymoon in June of 1958.

Chapter Sixteen

Steam Engines and Stick Shifts

Seeing New York on the Reader's Digest trip was both exciting and eye-opening, especially since, before my college days, I had never travelled outside of Maryland, except for a school trip to nearby Washington, D.C. My longest trip in those days was the one summer sojourn with my parents when I was 12 or so for a few days at Ocean City, Maryland's eastern shore beach of choice. Since my mom's family lived and worked in Baltimore, we made innumerable trips there, which is why mom bought a series of cheap used cars whenever we could afford it.

Early on, mom would drive the winding Baltimore-Annapolis Boulevard in our 1930s Chevrolet with me in the back seat. I do remember that it was a herky-jerky trip because of the winding bumpy roads and my mother's battle with the gear shift on the floor at every stop: brake—clutch—shift to stop; clutch and shift to start again, shift from first gear to second to third.

We went to Baltimore mainly to see her only sister, Aunt Bessie Carp, a shorter version of my mother, which allowed me to play with my cousin Ralph Carp, the closest thing to a brother I ever had. Our favorite game was "jumping on mothers and fathers," an invention that consisted of jumping off a window sill onto Ralph's bed. We couldn't play it long because the racket would rile up our mothers. It's a wonder we didn't break the bed since Ralph Carp, two years older than I, was chubby as a kid.

Our game took place on the third floor of my grandmother's brownstone row house on Brookfield Avenue, in the center of the city. Aunt Bess lived there until I was 9 or 10 with Ralph and her husband, Nate Carp, a one-time light weight boxer and saloon keeper, who was unfailingly kind to me. Uncle Nate is the one who said of Annapolis, "If you walk a block in any direction, you fall overboard."

It was from that brownstone at age three that I got my first mention in the press. I wandered off by myself and, blocks away, I was picked up by a policeman, who took me to his station. A

Baltimore Sun article of the next day reported what transpired. When the police tried to find out my name, and I couldn't tell them, they asked, "What does your mother call your father?" The *Sun* reported my answer: "'Honey' was the hopeful reply." My distraught mother tracked me down by calling police stations and found me, I am told, coolly enjoying a huge lollipop.

My Baltimore cousin, Ralph Carp, the closest thing to a brother I ever had.

The household on Brookfield Avenue was pretty morose. My grandmother, nee Molly Frommer, was ill all the time I knew her and slept on a bed in the darkened dining room of the first floor. I had to kiss her every time we arrived for a visit, and she seemed sad but happy to see me at the same time. She had been bedridden for years, suffering from diabetes and other ailments. My mother said the illnesses began the day my grandfather, bedridden because of an accident (resulting in business losses), became deeply depressed and killed himself with a bullet to the brain. My mother was a teenager at the time, but the suicide would always haunt her. This tragedy would repeat itself when my mother was 60 and committed suicide with an overdose of pills.

My maternal grandmother, Molly Frommer Wolf, was ill all the time I knew her. She passed away when I was nine. My maternal grandfather, Raphael Wolf, whose first name was anglicized to Ralph when I and two of my cousins were named in his honor.

While the house was gloomy, our visits had their bright side, such as trips to kid-friendly Druid Hill park with Ralph Carp; warm bagels unfailingly brought by my uncle Harry on Sunday mornings, which he would announce "special delivery for Ralph Crosby;" and visits to "The Shop." The Shop was the office of the Wolf family's plumbing business, started by my grandfather and carried on by my Uncle Sam, who lived at The Shop. Two things make The Shop most memorable to me: the miniature toilet in the window advertising the business and the old Baltimore Shot Tower directly across Fayette Street.

Originally known as the *Phoenix Shot Tower*, at just above 234 feet high it was the tallest structure in the U.S. when completed in 1828. Ralph Carp and I would chase each other around this old brick, cone shaped structure, and wonder what the Tower was for. As we would later learn, molten lead was dropped from a platform at the Tower's top into a vat of cold water at the bottom. Like rain drops, the lead drops would form into perfect spheres and solidify into shot (bullets) for pistols and rifles. (In my research for this book, I discovered the tower's link to Annapolis. Charles Carroll of Carrollton, the last surviving signer of the Declaration of Independence, laid the Tower's cornerstone.) The Tower remains today, sort of a sentry near Baltimore's downtown harbor district.

Of all my mother's cars, I remember most the large, green Hudson we owned when I was in high school because I got to drive it. I don't recall what year the car was, probably a 1940s model, but it was "modern" with the gear shift mounted on the steering wheel column. It was quite long compared to many of its contemporaries and a bear to park, especially for a neophyte driver. Mom seldom let me drive it by myself, but it certainly made the trip to Baltimore easier. I believe mom was working as a ticket taker at the Republic theater, two doors up Main Street, when we owned the Hudson, and when she quit the job, we said goodbye to the car. Without mom working, the upkeep of a car was a bit much of a luxury.

Except for trips to Baltimore, we had little need for a car in Annapolis. My dad didn't learn to drive until I taught him when he was in his early 50s and the U.S.N.A. sheet metal shop moved out of Bancroft Hall to the City's outskirts. Of course, up until then he could walk to work or anywhere else he wanted to go. Teaching my dad to drive using a stick shift was not an easy task, especially how to hold the car on a hill with clutch and gas pedal so you didn't have to use the brake. He used his best curse words when he continually stalled on the hills.

One thing I recall with lingering fear is driving the Hudson up narrow Main Street which, at the time, unbelievably, was two way with parking on both sides. At the wide bottom of Main Street there was plenty of room, but when you got past Francis Street, the road was originally made for horses, not cars. Thankfully, in the 1950s, Main Street became one way going up, and Duke of Gloucester Street became one way going down.

Driving to Baltimore became easier in 1940 with the opening of the Governor Albert C. Ritchie Highway, a multi-lane road with a straight shot between Annapolis and Baltimore. An hour trip up the old road suddenly became 35 minutes. The road was named after the 49th Governor of Maryland, who served a record four terms from 1920 to 1935 and who made two unsuccessful runs for the U.S. Presidency.

Riding the Rails

Sadly, there was neither a Ritchie Highway nor a car in the Crosby family when mom decided that her only child, age 10, with buck teeth protruding, needed braces. But there was no orthodontist in Annapolis. So, she found one in Baltimore, which meant a rocking train ride on the local "Toonerville Trolley," the

Baltimore and Annapolis Railroad line, which I likened to the tag line of a popular orchestra leader of the day: "Swing and Sway with Sammy Kay."

After the first few trips to the orthodontist, Dr. Meyer Eggnatz, mom let me take the trip by myself. I'd walk to the Bladen Street rail station, only five minutes from Main Street, a few blocks behind the State House, and catch the train to Camden Station in downtown Baltimore, (now the site of the Orioles' baseball stadium) cross the street and catch the number five street car to Park Avenue and Reed Street, and walk a block to the Medical Arts Building. That trip, which I did for four years, is indelibly imprinted in my mind.

While the cost of those trips were not exorbitant, when coupled with the orthodontist's fees it was a financial burden. The total fee for my braces was around $4,000, an astronomical sum for my parents. Except for a few cheap, couple of dollars "house dresses," the simple, cotton dresses worn for household chores and quick errands, mom got no new clothes during those four "braces" years. But, she never complained.

The Bladen Street rail station was the culmination of rail travel in Annapolis after the era when railroads were kings of transportation in the U.S. The reign of American railroads began in nearby Baltimore on July 4, 1828, when ground was broken for the Baltimore and Ohio Railroad (B&O), the first in the U.S. built for passenger travel as well as freight. Appropriately, because it was "Independence Day," the first stone, or cornerstone of the B&O was laid by the ubiquitous, 90-year-old Charles Carroll of Carrolton.

The first steam powered train came to Annapolis in the 1840s, ending at a depot on West Street at Calvert Street, just a block from Church Circle. The trains of the Annapolis and Elkridge Railroad would intersect with the B&O at a midway spot between Baltimore and Washington aptly named Annapolis Junction. In 1887, the Baltimore & Annapolis Short Line, providing travel between the two cities, opened with the station on Bladen Street. Both railroads were absorbed and electrified by the Washington, Baltimore and Annapolis Electric Railway, which operated until 1935, when the Great Depression and the rise of the automobile forced it to end passenger service.

Beginning in 1908, despite much grumbling by some citizens, the WB&A brought its trains right through downtown Annapolis, travelling down West Street, around Church Circle, to Market Space and back out again. Many arriving new midshipmen, such as my friend Bill Busik, remember the train dropping them off near the

Academy gate. The citizens' grumbling eventually grew to a roar because buildings shook and noise swelled as the trains passed and the traffic became snarled as auto use increased. So, several years after the railroad's franchise expired in 1932, the trains left the city's streets.

Death of the WB&A led to the formation of the Baltimore and Annapolis Railroad, which carried passengers like me between Bladen Street and Camden Station.

Annapolis' train saga was front and center in author William Oliver Stevens' book *Annapolis: Anne Arundel's Town*, published in 1937, just before my family moved to 183 Main Street. Author of more than 30 books, Stevens, who taught English at the Naval Academy for 21 years, knew his Annapolis travel. Here's an abridged version of how he begins his journey in *Annapolis: Anne Arundel's Town*:

> *One of the unique distinctions of Annapolis, the one that may strike the traveler even before he arrives there, is that this city is the one state capital in the nation which cannot be reached by a steam railroad. But it was not ever thus...." In the Good Old Days... there were two steam railroads. On one of them the startled passenger would have recognized no less a personage than Rudyard Kipling punching the tickets. At any rate, he was the identical image of Rudyard. Strangers, fascinated, would eye him during the entire journey from Baltimore, wondering if it really could be the author incognito, making an honest living on the railroad.... But despite the amazing resemblance—glasses, walrus moustache and all—you came to the reluctant conclusion that he must be someone else, for he spake neither in prose nor in verse. Only as a little train slid into the station at the end of the route he would open the door of the car and announce the name twice in a mild tone, the first with a rising inflection like a question, the second, as a reply: "Nap-liss? Napliss." He never varied this formula in thirty years.*
>
> *After the sooty trains had outlived their usefulness, both the lines took to electricity. One, the Washington route, even sent huge cars thundering through the streets of the Ancient City like some fearful Brontosaurus intent on its prey. Now, also like the Brontosaurus, the electric road has gone extinct, on account of small and more*

*nimble enemies; to wit, the automobiles. Its bones are
dust, its good rails rust, its soul is with the saints, we
trust...*

*The other railroad, the Short Line, still shuttles an
electric car back and forth from Baltimore, but how long
that will last, against what Henry Ford and General
Motors are doing, is a question. And, alas, Rudyard
Kipling is punching tickets no longer.*

The Short Line carried passengers until I was a sophomore in
high school in 1950. But the locomotive on the train I rode to see
the Baltimore orthodontist eschewed both steam and electricity for
diesel power.

By the way, it is from the opening chapter in Stevens' book that
my friend and noted photographer Marion Warren and his daughter
Mame got the subtitle of their wonderful photographic collection,
An Annapolis Portrait, 1859-1910, subheaded, "The Train's Done
Been And Gone," those words spoken in the vernacular, Stevens
wrote, by a railroad employee to an agitated man on the station
platform whose watch proved to be slow.

The Short Line made many stops between Annapolis and
Baltimore, giving residents of the small villages along the way
access to both cities. One of its first stops outside of Annapolis was
just across College Creek in West Annapolis, a location misnomer
since "West Annapolis" is north of the City. The train crossed
College Creek on a railroad trestle that evokes memories of my
teenage adventures to cross it on foot to meet some friends in the
woods of West Annapolis, six pack of ill-gotten beer in hand.

The careful walk on the ties across the trestle was somewhat
scary, but the danger of an oncoming train added to the seeming
danger. I say "seeming" because there were two escapes if a train
was coming: one, a side platform for workmen in the middle of
the bridge or, two, a jump into the creek from the fairly low trestle.
Since it took only a few minutes to cross the bridge, I never had to
use either escape, thank goodness.

The old West Street depot continued to service trains for
special purposes in the 1940s. One of those purposes was carrying
the Brigade of Midshipmen to Army-Navy football games in
Philadelphia.

Watching the mids marching out West Street to the train was an
annual Annapolis event in my youth. I remember my dad taking
me to the train station to see the big train and the brigade marching

to it. The year would have been either 1940 or 1941 because, when the brigade returned, their march took on a party-like atmosphere with the mids chanting the winning score and the crowd cheering and yelling. That's why I pinpoint those years; in 1942, the game was played in Annapolis; in '43 at West Point. For the next six years, Army won or tied.

Midshipmen marching up West Street to the train that would take them to the Army-Navy football game in Philadelphia. (Collection of the Maryland State Archives)

"Steam"

But it was the steamboat not the railroad that had the most effect on Annapolis. Not only did the steamboat play a critical role in ferrying goods and passengers to and from the capital port city, the development of steam technology helped bring the Naval Academy to Annapolis. Naval officers of the mid-1800s required a knowledge of how this technology affected naval warfare, so young officer candidates needed an education in steam mechanics and a place to learn about it. Enter George Bancroft and Fort Severn. In recent times, when the Navy was driven by diesel and nuclear power, midshipmen were required to take a course in thermodynamics. At the Academy, the course is nicknamed—"Steam!"

Even in the railroad years, steamboats remained a fast means of transportation on the Chesapeake Bay, as well as a popular tourist attraction. These ferries moved crops, freight and passengers within a network that connected towns and railroads on opposite sides of the Bay, making Annapolis again a booming port city in the early 20th century. There were wharves for docking ferries at the foot of both Prince George and King George Streets, in the area called Hell Point. Numerous businesses located in the area because of the cheap ferry transportation of freight. Before the Naval Academy bought up the Hell Point property between King George and Prince George Streets in 1941, Johnson's Lumber yard took up a huge space at the end of King George, where ferries supplied its wood.

Sailboat ferries have plied the Bay, the Severn and Spa Creek from Annapolis' earliest days. In fact, the Annapolis Ferry crossed the Severn River, where the Naval Academy now stands, from the late 1600s until 1887 when the first Severn River Bridge was built. Steamboats began to replace the Annapolis sailboat ferries in 1813, when the first steamboat to travel on the Bay, the *Chesapeake*, made an excursion between Baltimore and Annapolis.

Ferries became well-known local names, such as the Governor Albert C. Ritchie (highway honoree as well), The Harrington and the Emma Giles. An 187-foot-long side-wheel steamer, reminiscent of the more famous Mississippi steamboats, The Emma Giles made round trips between Baltimore and Annapolis on a regular weekly basis from 1887 to 1936 and took passengers to Tolchester Beach, Maryland, an Eastern Shore resort. In conversations with some of my older Annapolitan friends, such as Lester Trott, born in 1918, they fondly remembered leisurely, summer rides on the ferry and recalled the picnics, horse-racing and roller coaster rides at Tolchester.

The ferries are a dim memory to me since I didn't often venture into Hell Point in those preteen years, but some of my friends told of earning "big money" diving for coins when the ferries arrived in the late 1930s and early 1940s. Some kids claimed to make as much as five or ten dollars a day—far more than their parents earned—when passengers would throw them nickels and dimes to dive for. They claimed finding the coins, magnified by the water and floating slowly, was easy. They'd stick each coin in their mouths for safekeeping and surface to make another dive.

The money-making dives and steamboat excursions from Hell Point ended when congestion caused by vehicles waiting to board the ferries snarled downtown traffic. A new ferry terminal opened in 1943 at Sandy Point on the Bay, about ten miles east of Annapolis. I recall my excitement and anticipation when my mom drove onto the ferry for our trip across the Chesapeake on the way to Ocean City.

The ferry era ended in 1952, my senior year in high school, with the opening of the Chesapeake Bay Bridge, with its Annapolis area entrance near Sandy Point, allowing you to drive to the Eastern Shore. By the 1960s, the great steamboats had all but vanished from the Bay, replaced by majestic sailboats and expensive yachts coming to rest in Spa Creek in yet another Annapolis transformation, this time morphing the City into one of the nation's leading pleasure boating centers.

CHAPTER SEVENTEEN

"HI-YO SILVER! AWAY!"

Many an evening at 7:30 in the 1940s, I'd be lying on my stomach on the living room rug waiting in great anticipation for the familiar words and music to come out of the radio console:

> *Announcer:* "From out of the past come the thundering hoof beats of the great horse Silver! The Lone Ranger rides again!"

> *Actor:* "Come on, Silver! Let's go, big fellow! Hi-yo Silver! Away!"

It has probably been more than 65 years since I heard those words from the radio, accompanied by the inspiring, fast-paced music of Rossini's *William Tell Overture* that made you imagine a galloping horse, yet I can never forget the experience. It is etched in my memory and the memories of my generation as if they were burned there with a branding iron.

Who of my generation could ever forget the Lone Ranger's Indian sidekick Tonto, who referred to his partner as "Ke-mo-sah-bee;" the Lone Ranger's reliance on only silver bullets; or Tonto's horse Scout and Tonto's echo to "Hi-yo Silver! Away!"—"Git-em up, Scout!"

Introduced on the radio in 1933, the year I was born, the Lone Ranger was emblematic of entertainment in my years growing up when popular shows and personalities moved from radio to the movies, to television and even to comic books. Another hero who appeared on radio in 1933 was *Jack Armstrong, the Old American Boy,* a globe-trotting, high school age, adventurer, whose character also starred in a movie serial and a comic book. Also, one of my favorites was *The Shadow,* a crime-fighting vigilante, whose show-ending words became part of the American idiom: "The weed of crime bears bitter fruit. Crime does not pay…. The Shadow knows!" The

Shadow also appeared in magazines, comic strips and movies.

A number of my favorite radio singers of the 1930s and 1940s went on to even greater fame on television and in the movies, including Doris Day, Frank Sinatra and especially, Bing Crosby, perhaps the most well-known entertainer of the twentieth century. I can't count how many times, upon my introduction to new people, they would jokingly say, "Any relation to Bing?" I even used his name as a tool when someone seemed to mishear my name, I'd say, "Crosby, like in Bing." That was universally understood. Today Bing Crosby is mostly remembered around Christmas when his "White Christmas" song plays on the radio and his "White Christmas" movies play on TV. Bing's friend and favorite foil, Bob Hope, a great radio and TV comedian who did the musical comedy "Road" movies with Crosby, such as 1942's "Road To Morocco," was almost as popular an actor/comedian as Bing Crosby was an actor/singer. Hope is remembered today mostly as an Oscars' ceremony emcee. But Hope came into our lives on his own through radio and TV shows, movies and the special USO shows he did for soldiers overseas—as did Bing Crosby—and for which Hope was much honored.

While shows and celebrities bounded from one media to another, all were spawned by radio, the medium that branded my generation's childhood. Radio was not only our link to the world beyond Annapolis, it introduced us to a broader, more sophisticated and enlightened world and to the people who brought that world to life.

Besides radio and the movies, classic entertainments for adults of the late 1930s and early 1940s were dancing and card-playing. My parents went many Saturday nights to the Elks for the weekly dance with a live band, and in my teens I'd join them briefly for a soft drink and a dance with mom, which she enjoyed a lot more than I. Sometimes I would stay at the Elks Club to watch my mom and dad dance the last dance, for which the band always played "Good Night Sweetheart," a popular song of the 1930s and their favorite. My mom would sometimes sing the first verse of the song, another of our Bing Crosby favorites:

Goodnight sweetheart, 'til we meet tomorrow
Goodnight sweetheart, sleep will banish sorrow
Tears and parting may make us forlorn
But with the dawn a new day is born
So I'll say goodnight sweetheart, though I'm not beside you
Goodnight sweetheart, still my love will guide you
Dreams involve you and in each one I'll hold you
Goodnight sweetheart, goodnight

Dancing was widespread in clubs in Annapolis, as I'm sure it was all over the U.S.

Card-playing—especially Bridge, Hearts and Pinochle—were for home entertainment. My parents played Hearts with friends at the dining room table in our apartment, often into the late evening when I was in bed nearby listening to their chatter.

My mother taught me how to play cards at an early age as a way to pass the time when I was sick in bed, which was often in those days. In my childhood, illnesses were passed from child to child on a regular basis. I had the measles, mumps, chicken pox and, luckily, only minor cases of whooping cough and scarlet fever. While my case of scarlet fever was milder than most, I do remember the strange feeling of peeling away the top layer of the skin on my arms and stomach, a result of the disease.

The great illness fear of my childhood was polio. In my youth of the 1940s and early 1950s, poliomyelitis would paralyze or kill some 50,000 people each year in the U.S. Pictures of children in iron lungs, which helped them breath, bothered us youngsters but created deep fear in our parents. No one was immune, not even Franklin D. Roosevelt, who had become permanently paralyzed from the waist down in 1921.

It wasn't until 1955 that Jonas Salk's vaccine for polio prevention was made available and almost immediately thereafter polio cases were drastically reduced. In 1957, mass immunizations by the March of Dimes, which Franklin Roosevelt helped found, cut cases 90%.

While movie newsreels of the day showed children in iron lungs, the concern about polio or any other danger disappeared as the adventures of our movie heroes flickered on the silver screen.

My early heroes—dramatic and athletic—taught us a lot of good lessons—"Honesty is the best policy," "Help thy neighbor," "Crime does not pay!" In the movies, they taught us some bad lessons, too, such as how fashionable it was to smoke cigarettes and drink alcohol, that "The only good Indian is a dead Indian," and that the only place for black people was as servants. Just how insidious that could be came to me reading the comment of a classmate in a book of reminiscences for one of our high school reunions. He wrote: "It's funny how we never thought about segregation in those days. To us, it was just a given. I always thought the 'negroes' were there to do all our menial tasks."

Radio made us laugh at the antics of such comedians as Jack Benny, George Burns and Fibber McGee and Molly, and after World War II, the zany antics of the hugely successful comedy duo of Dean Martin and Jerry Lewis; it made us cry with such eye witness reports as the flaming crash of the German airship Hindenburg; it panicked millions of listeners in 1938 when Orson Welles broadcast a play about Martians invading earth that was mistaken for the real thing; and it thrilled us with broadcasts of popular football and baseball games and boxing bouts.

Before television, my dad and I would listen together to Army-Navy football games on radio. We also tuned into Joe Louis' heavyweight championship fights. Like millions of Americans, we were awed by the winning power of Louis, known as the "Brown Bomber." While my dad mouthed the racial prejudice of his south county roots, when it came to Joe Louis, who held the heavyweight crown from 1937 to 1949, dad was color blind. So was much of white America, which bought into Louis' image as an honest, hardworking fighter and patriot. Louis is considered the first African American to be a national hero.

While dad and I enjoyed listening or watching sports together on radio and TV and mom was interested in almost everything I did, neither of them ever watched me play sports, except for one basketball game in the St. John's gym when I was a pre-teen. Dad watched me shoot pool, but that's because the pool room was his usual stop on the way home from work. It didn't bother me when I was growing up, but it perplexed me in later years. I still wonder why? I'm sure dad was at work during many of those games, and mom wasn't interested in sports. Plus, in those days, I don't think many parents were as deeply involved in their children's games as we were later. Of the hundreds of lacrosse games my son Ray played over his pee wee league years through his club lacrosse years after college, I don't think I missed more than a dozen.

The exploits of another sports hero I listened to on Sundays in fall was "Slingin Sammy" Baugh, quarterback of the Washington Redskins pro football team from 1937 to 1952. It was fun in the front room imitating Baugh fading back and throwing one of his classic passes. He made the forward pass a great offensive weapon in the National Football League. I made throwing a rolled up towel dangerous to lamps and ash trays.

Musical Memories

Besides the big console radio in the front room, we had a small radio on the bureau beside the dining room table so mom could listen to music as she did her housework. One of radio's great appeals back then was the music it brought into the house, especially in a home like ours that had no phonograph. I distinctly remember when I was about 12 years old my mom standing at the ironing board, apron neatly tied around her house dress, hand wielding the iron like a see-saw, when a song came over the radio called "The Bluebird of Happiness," sung beautifully by the operatic tenor Jan Peerce. I heard it a number of times around then and, in my impressionable youth, it touched me, and it has stayed with me throughout life. In depressing times, I have often sung to myself some of the uplifting words of the song's refrain:

> Be like I, hold your head up high,
> Till you find a bluebird of happiness.
> You will find greater peace of mind
> Knowing there's a bluebird of happiness.
> And when he sings to you,
> Though you're deep in blue,
> You will see a ray of light creep through,
> And so remember this, life is no abyss,
> Somewhere there's a bluebird of happiness.

I hadn't heard that song since the 1940s until I played it when researching this book. It still thrills me. And it brought back memories of my mother standing at the ironing board, her wavy black hair framing her smiling face as she watched her young son sitting at the dining room table, enthralled by the music magically coming from that little box on the bureau.

Songs of my youth became some of the great popular American classics, such as: "Over The Rainbow," by Judy Garland; "Night and Day," by Frank Sinatra; bandleader Artie Shaw's rendition of "Stardust," "Sweet Georgia Brown," by the Mills Brothers, "April Showers," by Al Jolson, "If I Didn't Care," by the Ink Spots," bandleader Glenn Miller's "In The Mood," and Kate Smith's "God Bless America," as well as a bevy of songs by Bing Crosby and Nat King Cole.

Radio music's popularity was fostered by one show (later on TV as well) in the mid-1930s to the mid-1950s called "Your Hit Parade," which we listened to most Saturday evenings, especially during the World War II years. The show's format was to broadcast the country's most popular songs, ending the evening with the number one hit. Naturally, the first number one on the first episode was a Bing Crosby favorite called "Soon." Stars such as Frank Sinatra and Doris Day were regular singers on "Your Hit Parade."

However, one singer came on the scene that changed the direction of music. I recall playing the pinball machine in the Wardroom Restaurant on Main Street when this high-pitched, but pleasant voice came wailing out of the juke box, plaintively singing,

> *If your sweetheart sends a letter of goodbye,*
> *It's no secret you'll feel better if you cry.*

Given the pitch of the voice, I didn't know if the singer was male or female at the time, but he was soon all the rage. Johnnie Ray and his song "Cry" took the music world by storm in 1951. He followed up "Cry" with "The Little White Cloud That Cried," which branded him variously as the "Cry Guy," "The Nabob of Sob," and the "Prince of Wails," appropriate nicknames since he sang with great emotion.

Such emotional music had an impact on us teens in those high school years. I remember, amidst our penchant for jitterbugging, slow dancing to such sentimental songs as new singer Tony Bennett's first hit, "Because of You." After hearing Johnnie Ray's "Walking My Baby Back Home" on a date with a young lady in my senior year in high school, I remember humming that song to myself as I walked the mile from her house to Main Street, and such early 1950s songs have always reminded me of those wonderful discovering times of youthful romance. Perhaps the most romantic for me was the popular ballad of the mid '50s, "Young and Foolish," for it was the song much in vogue when I fell in love with my wife to be, Carlotta. (Tony Bennett's version of "Young and Foolish" became "our song," especially symbolic for me because its lyrics referred to my childhood melodic friend the "bluebird" of happiness. Tony Bennett reprised "Young and Foolish" in 1976, the year I moved our family to a house we built just south of Annapolis on a creek emanating from the South River, a location that couldn't be far from where my ancestor, Burden Crosby first brought his ship, the "George," to America in the early 1730s.)

Music aficionados consider Johnnie Ray's rhythm and blues style as the precursor of rock and roll. In fact, 1951 was the year "rock and roll" was first used to describe the new music, though it didn't erupt until later in the 1950s, led by the rise of Elvis Presley. But for my crowd in the early 1950s, the music of choice was R&B. It was the time that African-American blues and jazz began crossing over. What once had been called "race music," became universally accepted as "Rhythm and Blues," and was given its own category in the music bible, Billboard magazine. The music had great dance rhythm and was a bit sexually suggestive, which appealed to us teenagers. We danced to such songs as "The Huckle-Buck" and "Ain't That A Shame," the latter by Fats Domino, who would produce many memorable hits, such as one of my favorites, "Blueberry Hill."

Our gravitation to African-American music and musicians was spurred on by the attractions at Carr's Beach, just two miles across the Eastport Bridge from downtown Annapolis. Carr's Beach and its nearby sister beach, Sparrow's Beach, were major Chesapeake Bay resorts for African Americans that flourished in the 1940s and 1950s. They attracted thousands of visitors for swimming, picnics and the like, but the major claim to fame was the Carr's Beach Pavilion, one of the major stops on the "chitlin" circuit, an entertainment tour that catered to black audiences. On weekends in the summer, you might hear Fats Domino pounding out "Ain't That A Shame" at the pavilion, or hear such musical legends as Count Basie, Duke Ellington, Ella Fitzgerald, Billie Holiday and Lionel Hampton. While whites were welcome to join the audience at Carr's Beach Pavilion, we teenagers were a bit too intimidated, so we'd drive down the road close to the beach and sit in the car to listen to the music and the loud excitement that it produced. Some of my friends would drive their motorboats right up to the beach to listen.

Remembering the Movies

In my preteen years, the greatest musical influences were the singing cowboys, Gene Autry and Roy Rogers. I grew up watching them in one of the first great loves of my life—the Republic Theater. Since our apartment was separated from the Republic only by

Jenkins' stationery store, on Saturday morning I could lean out the front room window to gauge how long was the waiting line for the weekly cowboy movie. I could also read the marquee that jutted out over Main Street's sidewalk like the bow of a ship. Later, as an usher, I would climb a ladder to spell out the next attraction in big plastic letters on that marquee.

The Republic was an especially welcome respite on summer's really hot days because it was air-conditioned, something we lacked in our third floor apartment. However, we paid a price for a few hours of air-conditioning. The Republic's giant silver cooler was on the side of its building adjacent to my "back yard," and the noise loudly penetrated my back porch and my bedroom until the theater closed down at night.

The Republic was a small, dark, time-worn theater with a tiny balcony, but for me it was magical, made so by the moving pictures on the silver screen. If the radio connected us to the real world outside of our insular small town in the 1930s and 1940s, then motion pictures were our escape from that reality. Even during the depression, movies flourished, as fearful sometimes suffering, people sought escape from gloomy economic times. Movie houses dominated small towns in my youth, and tiny Annapolis had four theaters, the Republic; the Circle, only a block away on State Circle; and the Capital, about a half mile from Church Circle out West Street. In segregated Annapolis, blacks had their own movie house, the Star.

For us kids, movies supplied cheap, exciting entertainment. With fifteen cents, we'd get a ten-cent movie plus a serial and cartoon and a five-cent box of candy from the vending machine in the Republic's lobby. On Saturday morning, I'd get toward the head of the line, find the right cushioned seat in the middle of the theater, and with my Jujyfruits in hand and mouth, wait for the show. First, we'd get laughs watching a cartoon featuring such animated characters as Bugs Bunny, Popeye or Porky Pig. Then we'd get a thrill from a cliffhanger short serial, where the hero or heroine would be in a deadly trap at the end of each segment— think dangling on a rope above bubbling hot lava—only to be miraculously saved at the beginning of next week's segment. Of course, the idea was to bring us back next week, but we hardly needed coaxing. The serial I remember most was *Perils of Nyoka*, about a heroic, dare-devil, attractive, young lady with athletic and martial arts skills who faces down evil in the desert.

In my early years of movie-going, the films would likely feature

Gene Autry. There were many other cowboy B-Western movie heroes, such as Randolph Scott, Rocky Lane and Bob Steele, but Autry was the king, even though Roy Rogers would later be known as "King of the cowboys." It's hard to believe the influence that Gene Autry had in the late 1930s to the early 1950s.

The first of the singing cowboys, Autry's songs, including his signature "Back in the Saddle Again," flooded not only his movies, but his radio and television shows and live performances. He is still remembered at Christmas when you hear his renditions of "Here Comes Santa Claus," which he wrote, "Frosty The Snowman," and "Rudolph The Red-nosed Reindeer." Autry was so popular that even his horse "Champion" had radio and television series.

Naturally, B-Western cowboys shared the attributes of bravery, honesty, toughness and marksmanship. The entertainment value of music added luster to singing cowboy movies. That's why Roy Rogers succeeded so closely on the heels of Gene Autry. Rogers appeared in more than 100 films as well as his own radio and TV shows, often appearing with his wife, Dale Evans, and the singing group he started with, "The Sons of the Pioneers." The popular singing group recorded such classics as "Tumbling Tumbleweeds" and "Cool Water." Dale Evans, also a singer, wrote the Roy Rogers' theme song, "Happy Trails." Like Autry's "Champion," Rogers' horse "Trigger" was well known to us movie-goers.

I enjoyed both legends, Autry and Rogers, but my favorite was Hopalong Cassidy, a fictional cowboy who was a character in novels by Clarence E. Mulford. The character, played by actor William Boyd, was visually different than his singing contemporaries, which attracted me to his movies. His white hair and black suit and black hat would normally have branded him as the villain. But "Hoppy," as he was nicknamed, had all the virtues of his singing brothers.

William Boyd eventually bought the rights to the "Hoppy" character and films and took him to television, where the character became even more popular, making Boyd a multimillionaire.

I grew up in the golden age of movies. Of the American Film Institute's top ten greatest American films of all time, half were made from 1939 to 1952, including: #1 *Citizen Kane* (1941); #3 *Casablanca* (1942); #5 *Singin' In The Rain* (1952) #6 *Gone With The Wind* (1939); and #10 *The Wizard of Oz* (1939).

Humphrey Bogart's Casablanca is one of my personal favorites as are a bunch of other 1939-1952 top 100 films, including Bogart's *The Maltese Falcon* and *The African Queen*, and the great westerns,

Alan Ladd's *Shane* and Gary Cooper's *High Noon*. The latter offered great relief from the marching and training when it was shown while I was on a two week Naval Reserve boot camp at Maryland's Bainbridge Training Center in 1952. When you add such top 100 films as Jimmy Stewart's *Mr. Smith Goes To Washington* (1939) and *The Philadelphia Story* (1940), and Henry Fonda's *Grapes of Wrath* (1940), there's no question it was American films' golden age.

The end of that period was also the end of the dominance of radio and the movies in information and entertainment. All that radio and the movies had provided in the '30s and '40s could be found on television in the '50s.

TV Comes to Main Street

Although television had been invented in the 1930s—thus the TV button on our radio console—most Americans had not seen a TV show as 1950 dawned. Even in that year, only ten percent of the American people had TV sets.

At that time, whenever a city got a television station, movie theaters began to close. Those who didn't have a TV set visited relatives or friends who did so they could watch shows such as the Texaco Star Theater, featuring the unprecedentedly popular Milton Berle. The visitors liked what they saw and bought their own TV sets. My parents were among those buyers, purchasing that 12-inch Philco tabletop set in 1951. We laughed at Berle but laughed much harder when "I Love Lucy" came along. The show featured Lucille Ball and her real life husband, Desi Arnaz, playing a husband and wife whose hi jinx and marital mess ups were hilarious. By 1954, as many as 50 million Americans tuned in to "I Love Lucy."

At some point our tiny TV set, which sat on a stand in the dining room corner, acquired a "rabbit ears" antenna, so called because it resembled a pair of long ears on top of the television set. They were actually two metal rods that telescoped open when you pulled them. They improved TV signal reception, so how you positioned them determined the picture's quality, a critical factor since we received programs from both Baltimore and Washington channels. But even with rabbit ears, our pictures were often fuzzy. We watched anyway, fascinated that moving pictures, some of them live, could be captured out of thin air. Later, my dad affixed an antenna to the roof and increased the picture clarity fourfold.

Television not only reduced movie-going and radio listening, it changed the culture of our generation. No longer did we have to leave the house for theater entertainment nor get our news by just listening or reading. Television gave us home theater and news events we could actually see. And it was free! Television also reduced the parochialism of small towns like Annapolis. What we watched, millions of Americans were also watching, creating a mass culture that tied us together no matter where we lived. During the Army-McCarthy hearings, for instance, because they were televised, you could go almost anywhere in America and discuss with locals what was happening to Senator Joseph McCarthy.

Before television, the entertainment all kids had in common was comic books. I grew up in what has been called another "Golden Age" — this one of comic books, 1930-1950. Comic books became an industry of its own when Superman was created in 1938, birthing the super hero genre, followed by Batman in 1939. They were followed by such colorful (literally) heroes as Captain America, Captain Marvel, Plastic Man and Wonder Woman.

Comic books, which cost ten cents apiece, were not only fun to read, they were tradable, and I'd often take a stack around to Duke of Gloucester Street to a friend's house and barter my latest Supermans for her latest Batmans. My friend John Henneberger and I traded comic books, too, and once had the idea that we could pool our collection and sell them for a few cents apiece. As John said many years later, those comics would be worth thousands of dollars today. A copy of the inaugural Superman comic, "Action Comics No. 1," has sold for as much as $2.16 million. I'm sure one of us had a copy and sold it for a few cents.

Despite the comic book craze of grammar school years, I never stopped going to the library, especially after my junior year English teacher, Miss Davis, opened my eyes to fiction by the likes of Hemmingway, Fitzgerald and Steinbeck, all of whom fueled my writing desire. However, I must admit, I was drawn more deeply into the fictional world created by former comic book writer Mickey Spillane. Spillane's tough guy character, appropriately named Mike Hammer, first appeared in the book *I, The Jury*, published in 1947 and reissued in paperback in 1948. Filled with just revenge and sexual innuendo (and available in paperback for just fifty cents), *I, The Jury* grabbed the public's attention so tightly that Spillane followed it with multiple Mike Hammer novels, such as *My Gun Is Quick* and *Vengeance Is Mine*, which I read with great relish. Amid the great writers such as Hemmingway and Steinbeck, Mickey Spillane became the bestselling author of the first half of the 20th century.

Books that were supposed to have a life-altering effect on me didn't. When I read *Catcher In The Rye*, published in 1951, I couldn't' relate to the alienated, rebellious prep school fencing team manager who runs off to New York City and attends plays. While today I understand why it is a great novel, back then, I couldn't identify with its hero, Holden Caulfield. Later, I would feel similarly about another classic of the time, Jack Kerouac's *On the Road*. I read it with some understanding and empathy but not longing. The world of drugs and aimless travel and rebellion against conformity didn't appeal to the college crowd I had joined by then. Though I thought of myself as an individualist, I was, in fact, a conformist seeking a "good life," with family, job and affluence. Personal fulfillment would characterize my life, though there was also a reach for success—kind of an "I'll show you" attitude of the boy in the third floor apartment. I found that fulfillment in journalism with its front page bylines and, later, in the entrepreneurship of building businesses. I found out who I was in the 1950s, but there is no doubt, as Wordsworth wrote, "The child is father of the man."

CHAPTER EIGHTEEN

TOLERANCE AND INTOLERANCE

While I found out "who I was" in the 1950s, I'm sure that my childhood before that defined my character, socially and spiritually. While I found great joy in those growing up years, it was not always a pleasant journey. The unpleasantness came when tolerance was followed by intolerance. My parents' interreligious marriage, which originally caused my mother's banishment from her family, was met with eventual tolerance from both sides of the family—my mother accepted by the Crosbys and my father embraced by the Wolfs. But outside of the family their marriage often produced intolerance, for my mother from both Jews who disdained mixed marriages and from prejudiced gentiles that abounded in Annapolis. For me, as I was growing up, the narrow-mindedness came from several directions including, surprisingly, from the churches of both my mother and my father.

The history of my state, Maryland, is somewhat analogous to our family experience. Cecil (Cecilius) Calvert, Lord Baltimore, founded the Maryland Province in 1634, following the successful efforts of his late father, George, to obtain a charter from King Charles I of England. Like his father, Cecil was Catholic, which would cause difficulties in England, then dominated by the Anglican Church.

The Calverts saw this Maryland Colony not only as a source of income but as a haven for Catholics fleeing the discrimination of Anglicans.

To support religious toleration between Protestants and Catholics, Cecil Calvert told colonists traveling to Maryland to leave religious rivalries behind, told his colony managers to ensure religious peace, and implored his fellow Catholics to practice their faith discreetly.

For a while, the colonists practiced toleration voluntarily. Then, in 1649, several events supported toleration and, at the same time, interrupted it. First, seeking more settlers to the new colony, Maryland's governor invited persecuted Puritans in Virginia to settle in Maryland, some of whom chose Severn River land far north of the Catholic-oriented capital of the Colony, St. Mary's. Meanwhile, at St. Mary's, the Maryland General Assembly passed *An Act Concerning Religion*, known as the "Toleration Act," mandating religious toleration for all Trinitarian Christians—thus giving both Protestants and Catholics religious freedom. Looking for a more central location and to avoid the stridency of Catholics in St. Mary's City, Maryland's General Assembly moved the capital from St. Mary's City to Annapolis, formerly Anne Arundel Towne, in 1695, bringing with it the new Toleration Act.

This Act was far ahead of its time, but it didn't last long. In 1654, the act was repealed by Protestants, then in power, who passed a new law barring Catholics from openly practicing their religion.

Shortly after repeal of the Toleration Act, intolerance turned into war, the Battle of the Severn. As noted earlier, England's religious battles between Catholics and Protestants caused Governor William Stone, to require all colonists to take an oath of allegiance to the Catholic proprietor, Lord Baltimore. The settlers from Virginia who came to Maryland for religious freedom, refused to take the oath. Governor Stone ordered his soldiers to enforce his rule, but the settlers, outnumbered but more determined, defeated the Governor's troops. In an eventual truce, the Governor traded religious tolerance in exchange for recognition of Lord Baltimore's rule.

But while Maryland's religious toleration had brought various Christian sects to the Colony, it didn't promise toleration for all comers. If you denied the Holy Trinity or the divinity of Jesus, you could be executed or stripped of your wealth. In repealing the act, overzealous Puritans turned Catholics, Jews, Quakers and Atheists into second class citizens. These citizens could not vote, hold office or openly practice their religion.

Into this intolerant world was born Charles Carroll of Carrollton, on whose Spa Creek property I played as a youth. Though barred from holding public office in his formative years, he became integral to the American Revolution and the country's eventual religious toleration. That was quite an accomplishment considering that his father, Charles Carroll of Annapolis, almost left Maryland permanently when, in 1763, the legislature taxed the land of Catholics at a rate twice that of Protestants. The elder Carroll owned 40,000 acres. But the Carrolls pressed on, always honoring their religion. Just before his death, Charles Carroll of Carrollton summed up his life thusly:

*I have lived to my ninety sixth year; I have enjoyed
continued health, I have been blessed with great wealth,
prosperity, and most of the good things which the world
can bestow—public approbation, esteem, applause; but
what I now look back on with the greatest satisfaction to
myself is, that I have practiced the duties of my religion.*

Carroll of Carrollton's cousin, Charles Carroll the Barrister,
though a Protestant due to his father's conversion from Catholicism,
helped draft Maryland's first new constitution in 1776, which
included religious toleration for Catholics. This "Declaration of
Rights and Form of Government for the State of Maryland" included
a clause proclaiming "it is the duty of every man to worship God
in such manner as he thinks most acceptable to him; all persons,
professing the Christian religion, are equally entitled to protection
in their religious liberty; wherefore no person ought by any law
to be molested in his person or estate on account of his religious
persuasion or profession, or for his religious practice."

Both Carrolls' actions were prelude to passage of the First
Amendment to the U.S. Constitution in 1791, which prohibited
the making of any law restricting "the free exercise" of religion.
Admittedly, however, Maryland was slow to respond to the First
Amendment, keeping the Christian religion as a test for public
office until it passed the Constitution of 1867.

Intolerance Comes Home

Freedom of religion doesn't mean freedom from intolerance or
bigotry, as my family discovered. My mother and I never faced
discrimination on the scale suffered by the Puritan colonists or
Catholic Carrolls, but intolerance was ever present. I must admit,
my first experience with intolerance was my own childish stupidity.
On Conduit Street, just a few doors from the Carroll Barrister
House, was a Chinese laundry. When I was a kid of seven or eight, I
and some friends would taunt the Chinese shopkeeper with hateful
words: "Chinka Chinka Chinaman, eats dead rats..." Frustrated
and angry, he would chase us away from his door, yelling in
Chinese, and we'd laugh. While I can chalk it up to the ignorance
of youth, I still regret it. One of my partners in this "crime" against
the Chinese laundry man was my childhood friend Eugene Lerner,
whose father owned the Main Street pawn shop. Later in life,
Gene humorously reminded me of our mischief, though I know the

experience bothered him as much as it did me, especially since he became a respected judge, noted for his tolerance.

My mother felt the sting of intolerance when she moved to Annapolis, and it continued throughout her life. There was a time, when I was in college, she began receiving hate mail with invectives such as "dirty Jew" and "Jew bastard." We suspected these letters were from a woman in the Daughters of America group to which my mother belonged and, I believe, was its only Jewish member. I'm not surprised she joined a non-Jewish group. She had few Jewish friends. She always felt most of the town's Jewish ladies looked down their noses at her because of her "unkosher" marriage, especially to a workman who didn't own a business or own real estate, as many of their husbands did. In my dad's circle of friends there certainly were no Jewish men with wives to form a kinship with my mother. We never discovered the identity of the hate letter writer, but my mother quit the group, and the letters stopped. But the letters had done their damage. Those letters devastated my mother, and I believe they played a part in her recurrent depression, which ultimately led to her suicide.

While growing up in Annapolis, I faced no penalties such as those Charles Carroll of Carrollton faced when he was growing up in Annapolis, but you only had to go to the popular swimming beach Oak Grove, just below Annapolis on the South River, for stark evidence of intolerance that confronted me when I went as a youngster. In front of the beach entrance was a big sign with the Oak Grove name and these words:

"No Colored, No Jews, No Dogs Allowed."

This was literally a sign of the times. Annapolis historian and author Jane McWilliams recalls that when she was a child in the 1940s she saw a rental sign on an apartment in the Eastport area that read "Gentiles only need apply." She remembers asking what the word "Gentiles" meant. Antisemitism was on the rise when I was a youth due to the ascension of Adolf Hitler in Germany and, here in the U.S., openly antisemitic radio broadcasts by a Catholic Priest, Charles Coughlin. The controversial Father Coughlin, an avid supporter of Hitler's anti-Jewish policies, had millions of supporters and listeners and was only silenced by the Roosevelt Administration after the outbreak of World War II.

In the late 1930s, we heard about persecution of the Jews in Germany, but it wasn't until the war was ending when allied troops liberated the concentration camps that we saw photos and films of starved, skeletal camp victims and mass graves strewn with withered dead bodies. For me, the horror of the Holocaust wasn't just because half my family was Jewish, but even at 12 years old I knew Hitler's "final solution" was unfathomable inhumanity.

Even I had been unaware of the ubiquitous discrimination against Jews in America until I saw the movie "Gentleman's Agreement" when I was 14 or 15. This 1947 film, based on a popular novel, exposed rampant antisemitism among employers, hotels, social clubs, elite schools, resorts and beaches. If not excluded totally from such institutions, Jews faced quotas to restrict their numbers. That movie helped raise awareness of the evils of antisemitism throughout the country.

Despite such flagrant intolerance as Oak Grove's signs, Jews were prominent citizens in Annapolis in my youth. There were few Jewish families in Annapolis before the late 19th and early 20th centuries, when European pogroms, massacres of helpless Jews, caused many to flee to the U.S., including a number to Annapolis (and including my Wolf family ancestors, the Frommers and the Soloveitchiks, to Baltimore.) These Annapolis immigrant settlers, many of them craftsmen or merchants, set up their own businesses on Main Street, Market Space and West Street and lived above their stores. Certainly these Jews felt the sting of discrimination in Christian-dominated Annapolis, but by the time of my youth, the 1930s to the 1950s, they had become the successful merchant and professional class of the City and the downtown's major landlords who owned much of the real estate on Main Street. The children of many of these merchants—the Lerners, the Hyatts, the Wolods, the Wollmans, the Greenfields—were my friends.

I made some of these friends in Hebrew School, which I attended for a short time at the urging of my mother, even though she didn't attend the local synagogue. I even attended the synagogue until a series of events changed my religious direction. First, when I heard that the young males in attendance would have the honor of sipping ceremonial wine at Friday night services, I anxiously awaited my turn. But it never came. Second, there was resistance to my joining the local Jewish youth club. When I asked some friends why I was being excluded from these opportunities, they told me I was not Jewish enough. Even though in Jewish law a baby's religious identity is determined by its mother even if the father is gentile, which appears to have been arbitrary in my case at the Annapolis synagogue.

In looking back now on this rejection, it reminds me of the experience of Frank McCourt, renowned author of *Angela's Ashes*, who as a child in Ireland was rejected as an altar boy in his Catholic church because of his Protestant father. Intrafaith intolerance seemed to follow my mother until she died. When I asked the local rabbi to officiate at my mother's funeral, he refused, apparently because she wasn't a member of his Orthodox congregation. A Jewish friend got his reform rabbi from a county synagogue to preside at the funeral.

Angered by the slights to her young son, my mother said I didn't have to return to the synagogue if I didn't want to. I never returned. Later in my youth I began searching for faith and thought I'd try my father's family church, Calvary Methodist, to see how Christianity was practiced. The church was a beautiful building on State Circle across the street from the State House. During my short time attending services there, I heard talk of how the Jews killed Christ. That didn't sit too well, especially when some kids told me it meant that Jews didn't go to heaven.

Some years later, while in college, I joined what I thought was a more ecumenical congregation, the Annapolis Unitarian Church and even edited its newsletter. That experiment ended when I wrote an editorial for the newsletter on "Why can't dogs go to heaven?," questioning the idea of a heaven in the clouds. The Unitarian Church elders were not pleased. I wasn't pleased with their reaction, so we parted ways.

A Spiritual Journey

This memoir isn't about my search for faith, though that search informed my youth. But, I leave the subject with two observations on my spiritual journey.

First, my journey has been ecumenical. Besides having a Jewish mother and a Methodist father, I willingly married a Catholic and helped raise our children Catholic as I promised. That ecumenical journey had its benefits, too. In my youth, my Baltimore uncles would give me money gifts on Hanukkah, and my Annapolis family gave me Christmas gifts. In deference to my dad, my mother celebrated Christmas as a holiday as well, with all the trappings—a tree, gifts, cookies and a special dinner. That's one time I got the best of both religious worlds.

Second, while I abandoned all formal religions, in my youth I thought of myself as more Jewish than anything else—not because of beliefs, not because of training, and certainly not because the Jewish community accepted me—but because of my mother's family. From my Baltimore uncles there was always that admonition, "From a Jewish mother comes a Jewish child."

So when I entered college, I checked "Hebrew" on the orientation questionnaire. But even that remnant of my childhood slowly disappeared as I became exposed to literature, philosophy and history at the university. I became aware of the atheists, agnostics and searchers in the world, and I searched for my place in the pantheon of beliefs. I found no absolute truth for me, but I found a guide in a poem I have kept framed on my dresser for all of my adult life. Here's the poem, titled "Heresy," by Ella Wheeler Wilcox:

> The world has a thousand creeds, and never a one have I;
> Nor church of my own; though a million spires are pointing the way on high.
> But I float on the bosom of faith, that bears me along like a river;
> And the lamp of my soul is alight with love, for life, and the world, and the Giver.

Later in life, as my search continued, I have been guided by the words of two religious leaders I have had the good fortune to call my friends. One, the noted author and Christian philosopher Os Guinness, defined the search thusly:

> We are all distinct individuals who are at different stages on the journey. For some the road is simple; for others it is tortuous. When Peter Drucker was asked by fellow business consultant Ken Blanchard why he had become a Christian, he answered simply, "Because there's no better deal." For some the outer journey is hard enough, for others the inner journey may prove even more strenuous and long. But for all of us the invitation stands: To set out on the most important journey of our lives—from the understanding to the will and the will to action— bringing us to that place of faith in God that is the first step toward home.

Another friend and faith leader, Doug Holladay, defined my tortuous journey with a trapeze analogy. You are swinging from one trapeze to the other, he said, and when you successfully grab the second trapeze, it's a difficult but successful leap to faith. So far, I've only got a finger on the second trapeze, and I'm still trying for the grab.

Religion, I'm sorry to say, has created many a tortuous journey, some of it actual torture by zealots. But there's a deeper message in the Oak Grove sign. It's primary target was "No Colored..." No matter how much historic religious intolerance and early-to-mid-20th century antisemitism existed in Annapolis, both paled in comparison to discrimination against African Americans, undisguised bias that existed throughout the country, especially in the South. As my Jewish friend Lou Hyatt, legendary Annapolis entrepreneur, said to me, "Jews felt the sting of discrimination, but for blacks it was more like a mauling."

Chapter Nineteen

Annapolis' Racial Journey:

From Kunta Kinte to Thurgood Marshall

Searching for his family's progenitor in America, noted black author Alex Haley found that ancestor at the Annapolis City Dock. His name was Kunta Kinte, and he arrived in Annapolis on September 29, 1767, in the fetid hold of the slave ship *Lord Ligonier*. Kunta Kinte was one of the 98 survivors of 140 men and women abducted from Africa and imprisoned on the *Lord Ligonier*. Haley envisioned the way his 17-year-old Gambian ancestor would have been beaten, chained and dragged aboard that slave ship in the author's Pulitzer Prize-winning book *Roots*. As the "big canoe," as Kunta Kinte called the ship, sailed into Spa Creek and docked at the foot of Church (Main) Street, Haley imagined how the "toubob" (white men) prepared the frightened, weakened slaves for departure:

> Wielding their long-handled brushes once again, the toubob ignored the men's screams as they scrubbed the encrusted filth from their festering bodies, and the chief toubob moved down the line sprinkling his yellow powder. But this time, where the muscles were rubbed through deeply, he signaled for his big assistant to apply a black substance with a wide, flat brush. When it touched Kunta's raw buttocks, the rocketing pain smashed him dizzily to the deck.
>
> As he lay with his whole body feeling as if it were on fire, he heard men howling anew in terror, and snapping his head up, he saw several of the toubob engaged in what could only be preparing the men to be eaten. Several of them, in pairs, were pushing first one chained man and then the next into a kneeling position where he was held while a third toubob brushed onto his head a white

frothing stuff and then, with a narrow, gleaming thing,
raked the hair off his scalp, leaving blood trickling down
across his face.

Haley says the slaves then were taken to shore to what would become Annapolis' Market Space and placed in a holding house until the October 7 slave auction advertised in Anne Catherine Green's *Maryland Gazette*. While slaves brought to Annapolis were usually sold on the ships that brought them or in a shop or tavern, Alex Haley took creative license in his description of a slave sale at the harbor. Here's Haley's vision of how Kunta Kinte would have been sold into slavery:

> *"Top prime—young and supple!" The toubob shouted. Kunta was already so numb with terror that he hardly noticed as the toubob crowd moved in more closely around him. Then, with short sticks and whip butts, they were pushing apart his compressed lips to expose his clenched teeth, and with their bare hands prodding him all over—under his armpits, on his back, his chest, his genitals. Then some of those who had been inspecting Kunta began to step back and make strange cries.*
>
> *"Three hundred dollars!... three fifty!" The shouting toubob laughed scornfully. "Five hundred!... six!" He sounded angry. This is a choice young nigger! Do I hear seven fifty?"*
>
> *"Seven fifty!" came a shout.*
>
> *He repeated the cry several times, then shouted "Eight!" until someone in the crowd shouted it back. And then, before he had a chance to speak again, someone else shouted, "Eight fifty!"*

Thus, for $850 Haley says Kunta Kinte was sold to a Virginia planter to join the thousands of other Africans who worked the fields of tobacco, cotton and rice of the south. From the mid-17th century to the mid-18th century, Maryland was the second-largest slave-holding American colony. Much of Annapolis' early wealth was built on the slave trade. In the two decades before the American Revolution, at least 600, or one-third of those living in Annapolis were slaves. But their numbers must have paled compared to the number of slaves in the tobacco fields outside of the City.

It's hard for me to believe that Spa Creek, which brought me so much joy swimming, crabbing and fishing as a youth would be the 18th century scene of so much agony and inhumanity.

Segregated Annapolis

The separation of the races, one ultimate outgrowth of the slave trade, in my youth was blatant around City Dock, site of ancient slave sales. At the foot of Main Street, next to the Amoco gas station on the circle above City Dock stood the City's public restrooms, small red brick buildings with signs above the doors that read "White Men and Women" on one building and "Colored Men and Women" on the other.

Though I don't recall it, the Capital newspaper reported that a doctor with an office near the downtown hospital on Franklin Street "hung a shingle that read 'Blacks Tuesdays and Thursdays; Whites Mondays, Wednesdays and Fridays.'"

The Annapolis of my youth was so segregated racially, Maryland could have bordered Mississippi rather than Pennsylvania. As races, we learned to live separately, most of us neither embracing nor encroaching on each other's territory. I never went to school with a black person, not in grammar school, not in high school, not even at the University of Maryland. We didn't eat in the same restaurants or go to the same movie house. Black people had their own movie house in Annapolis, the Star Theater. Even my beloved library, in Reynolds Tavern, was off limits to blacks. Blacks didn't get their own—separate—Annapolis library branch until 1940.

I did mix with black kids, mostly at arm's length. I felt I was friendly with the black boys that racked the balls in Pap's pool room. I had an easy rapport with a rack boy named Richard, who liked to watch me shoot and would occasionally show a rooting interest in my game. It's telling that I never knew Richard's last name, and when we would occasionally pass on the street, our greetings were subdued nods of the head.

Occasionally, I would play ball with black kids, some pickup basketball or football on St. John's field, but those were not friendships. A few of my contemporaries built true friendships with black kids. My friend Pip Moyer's basketball skills gave him acceptance among the best black players, such as Joseph "Zastrow" Simms, whose friendship with Pip would surface importantly in later years when Martin Luther King, Jr. was assassinated.

The football field at St. John's was one of only two places I felt racial tension, personally, as a kid. A group of us white youngsters played a football game with a black kids' team on St. John's creekside field. I was running around as if I knew what I was doing in the homemade football pants my mother sewed from some cutoff, threadbare long pants. I remember they were navy blue, and I fantasized that they were Navy Midshipmen football pants. On the field that day I was awakened from my fantasy by a couple of black kids who clipped me from behind when the play was over. I said "nice block," even though I knew it wasn't a legal block, and they laughed. I don't know if their football transgression was racially motivated or out of disdain for this white kid running around in handmade football pants. And I don't know if the intimidation I felt had anything to do with race or just a fear of confronting two other boys. In the years after those racially mixed sandlot games until adult tennis games, I never played sports against—or with—a black person.

The one time I felt real racial intimidation happened when my friend Tommy Steward and I, about age 15, went to a Washington Senators' baseball game on a bus by ourselves. Being dropped off some blocks from Griffith Stadium in Washington, D.C., in an all-black neighborhood, the glares of black men on the streets were scary, and seemed to us to be filled with anger for two white youngsters invading their turf. The glares may have been our imagination, but the alarming feelings were not.

My closest relationships with African Americans as a youth were when I delivered papers to their homes in the small black enclave at the end of College Avenue and around the corner on Hanover Street. The interaction with those black families was no different than with my white customers, though I recall thinking their homes were more bedraggled and had a different smell to them. I thought the odor had something to do with race, though undoubtedly it was from food smells I wasn't used to. Of course, back then I didn't realize that our home had a different smell to others.

The College Avenue/Hanover Street enclave where I delivered papers was one of several black living areas outside of what one black writer called the "Harlem of Annapolis," a neighborhood in the Fourth Ward surrounding Clay Street, just a long block off of West Street where the old WB&A train tracks ran. In the early-to-mid 20th century, the neighborhood functioned as a city within the City with its own businesses and professionals—restaurants, food stores, tailors, dry cleaners, hair dressers and barbers, an undertaker, doctors and lawyers, and several churches. The neighborhood also boasted the Star Theater, dance halls and night clubs that drew the same talent as Carr's Beach—Pearl Bailey, Duke Ellington and Ella Fitzgerald among them. It was a neighborhood I ventured into when I worked for the Cohen's newspaper delivery company—collecting past due accounts—and one summer as a helper on construction of a low income housing project in Obery Court off Clay Street. While the residents were generally poor, the neighborhood was vibrant with music and playful banter throughout the day, and I felt little intimidation, except occasionally when trying to collect money from recalcitrant newspaper customers, but that happened with white customers as well.

The Star Theater was owned by the Eisensteins, one of many Jewish families serving the black community. The West Street area adjacent to the Clay Street neighborhood was full of Jewish merchants, especially clothiers and shoe stores, who would sell to blacks when other white merchants would not. Most city clothing and shoe stores would not let blacks try on clothes. A number of Jewish merchants not only operated stores but lived among their black customers in apartments above their stores. Having been discriminated against for so long, many Jews felt a kindred spirit toward African-Americans.

Philip L. Brown, the African-American author of *The Other Annapolis, 1900-1950,* a history of blacks in Annapolis, and coiner of the "Annapolis Harlem" phrase, explained:

> *Jews and colored residents of Annapolis got along well together, enjoying, in general, a friendly relationship. There existed a rapport between colored and Jews that was not present among colored and Gentiles. They both had experienced oppressions at the hand of Gentiles and were still being subject to discrimination.*

Greek immigrants who owned sit down restaurants on that area of West Street were likewise open-minded and were among the first to serve blacks.

When my mother would take me to Greengold's West Street clothing store for dungarees we'd often encounter some Clay Street residents shopping. Greengold's extended credit to black and white alike.

Beyond "Annapolis Harlem" and the homes on College Avenue/ Hanover Street several other black enclaves existed in downtown Annapolis, two near the City Dock. One was in Hell Point next door to Naval Academy Gate One, and in the 1930s it was a potpourri of blacks, whites and Filipinos who worked at the Academy or in the seafood industry. Their homes, often ramshackle without running water, electricity or heat, were acquired by the Naval Academy in 1941 for its further expansion. Several of the home-owning residents of the property, given only a few months to move out, were particularly chagrined when the property went undeveloped for years.

The second African American enclave near City Dock centered on Pinkney and Fleet Streets. Pinkney Street began just past Middleton Tavern which, as Mandris' restaurant, was flanked by a bar and pool room catering to African-Americans. Paralleling Pinkney was Fleet Street, more of an alley, both featuring decaying clapboard houses when I walked these streets as a youth. Pinkney had been an important maritime business street in colonial days. It was home to Horatio Middleton's father-in-law, Asbury Sutton, who owned the ferry inherited by Middleton that transported such Revolutionary war heroes as Washington, Jefferson and Tilghman.

Many of the Pinkney and Fleet Street homes are small, built for working-class people, especially seafood workers. As with the other Hell Pointers of the day, the Pinkney and Fleet Street residents—most of them black—lived there because that's where jobs for African Americans existed, mainly at the nearby Naval Academy or in the seafood houses shucking oysters, picking crabs and dressing fish.

The Chesapeake Bay had long been an employment haven for blacks. Slaves who gained their freedom in colonial times often turned to the Bay for work as well as sustenance. Following the Civil War, African Americans became some of Annapolis' most successful watermen, mostly in the booming oyster industry. At the turn of the twentieth century, among the ten oyster packing companies in Annapolis, was the Colored Union Oyster Packing Company on City Dock, packaging and selling the oyster catch of black watermen.

As segregation surged in Annapolis in the early 20th century (the Ku Klux Klan brought its white robes, fiery crosses and bigotry to Annapolis in the 1920s), many blacks moved to African-American communities outside the City, mainly to the outer West Street suburb of Parole. As Jane McWilliams observed in her definitive history, *Annapolis—City on the Severn*:

*The four decades before the Second World War saw
Annapolis' black citizens pushed further and further away
from mainstream city life. What happened in Annapolis
merely echoed policies and attitudes of other cities,
especially those in the south. In the next half century, all
of them, including Annapolis, would be held to account.*

While race relations in Annapolis were without major incident
in the 1930s into the late 1940s, during my high school years ('48-
'52) African American unrest became palpable. Black men who
had served in World War II realized that the expectation of equality
upon their return was a false promise, and they began to chafe under
continued discrimination. President Harry Truman struck a blow
against discrimination when, in 1948, he issued an executive order
desegregating the military, stating that "It is hereby declared to be
the policy of the President that there shall be equality of treatment
and opportunity for all persons in the armed services without
regard to race, color, religion, or national origin." The military
resisted this order, but when the Korean War came it brought full
integration when heavy casualties forced segregated units to merge
for survival.

In Annapolis, as the 1950s began, separation of the races
was still prevalent, but it was beginning to crack. While most
restaurants would not serve blacks, the Little Campus on Maryland
Avenue, owned by my friend Angie Nichols' family, following the
precedent set by Greek immigrant restaurants on West Street, in
1954 began serving African Americans after being integrated by a
black student from nearby St. John's College.

In the late 1950s, my boyhood hangout, Read's drug store
across from 183 on Main Street, began serving African Americans
at its lunch counter. By the end of the 50s decade, the local chapters
of the National Association for the Advancement of Colored People
(NAACP) and the Congress of Racial Equality (CORE) began
organizing protests against segregation.

A seminal event in Annapolis desegregation occurred on
November 25, 1960. Supported by the NAACP and CORE, five
leading Annapolis African American citizens staged what had
become the key integration technique, the "sit-in" demonstration,
at the bus station's Terminal Restaurant and waited to be served.
They were refused and arrested by the local police for trespassing.

The resulting picketing by African Americans and their white
supporters lasted two days before the Terminal Restaurant gave in,

accepting integration. The Terminal Restaurant's capitulation had a domino effect. The nearby Little Tavern on West Street, one of my high school haunts for a burger breakfast on the way to school, right away began accepting black customers, and a number of other Annapolis restaurants followed suit.

In the years that followed, as the battle over segregation raged across the country, I became friendly with three African Americans who had a great impact on civil rights in Annapolis—physician and political force Dr. Aris T. Allen; telecommunications entrepreneur and champion of African-American history Leonard A. Blackshear; and civic activist Joseph "Zastrow" Simms.

Aris Allen

I became friendly with Aris Allen very late in his life. We had become acquainted through some community activities, but it wasn't until 1989 the acquaintanceship blossomed when he asked for my assistance on his biography, *Achieving the American Dream*, which was being written by Jude Thomas May. Aris and I spent considerable time together discussing the book and its distribution, and he asked me to proofread the galleys. A tall, distinguished-looking gentleman—and I mean the latter in every sense of the word—Aris Allen exuded an aura of self-restraint and humility, despite his many accomplishments.

While he had achieved national fame as the first African-American to serve as presiding secretary of the Republican National Convention of 1980, Aris Allen's entire life was distinguished by accomplishment. He had risen from a hardscrabble youth as laborer, bus boy and elevator operator who didn't finish high school to night school student, Howard University graduate and Howard Medical College-trained physician.

When Aris came to Annapolis to practice medicine, black women were prohibited from delivering babies at the local hospital in the Annapolis Emergency Hospital (where I was born), and black physicians were denied the privilege of serving on the hospital's medical staff. Dr. Allen made arrangements to deliver black women's babies at their homes. When the mother needed hospital care, he would drive them to Washington in his own car—day or night. If Dr. Allen's patient had a non-obstetrical problem that required hospitalization, he had to turn the patient over to a white physician to be treated in a segregated section of the hospital.

Segregation at the local hospital continued until some young, white physicians began to include Aris in their deliberations and, with their support, in 1950 he became one of the first black doctors accepted on the hospital staff.

As his stature in the community grew, Aris was respected and consulted by Annapolis' white leaders, and he was asked to run for public office. Amid the racial unrest of the 1960s, Aris Allen was elected to the Maryland House of Delegates in 1966. His was always the voice of reason in racial matters. As Jude Thomas May wrote in Aris' biography:

> *While Aris strongly opposed the rules of segregation, he was understanding of some of those people who held these beliefs. He found it difficult to accept the attitudes of some extremists who argued that all whites were "devils". Instead, he believed many of them to be acting out a set of behaviors to which they had been conditioned from youth—no more or no less than this. Even the most vocal racist, he often related, was a human being with beliefs and feelings not unlike others. He, too, often had a family and children and a home.*
>
> *These views influenced the tactics which Aris followed and urged on his colleagues. Bigotry, however despicable, must be met with patience and understanding. Bigotry should not be met with bigotry. Should it be opposed? By all means! But, the opposition should be carefully guided by the realization that the opponents were also human beings, and therefore were capable of change. This was the key to his philosophy as well as his strategy.*

Aris' balanced approach to political issues, including race, attracted the attention in national Republican circles, so much so that he was tapped to run as Lieutenant Governor of Maryland on the gubernatorial ticket of J. Glenn Beall, Jr. Though defeated in his run for Lieutenant Governor, Aris became a member of the Maryland Senate and participated in national political events, culminating at the 1980 Republican National Convention.

One key role was as chair of the Progressive Republican Assembly, the party leadership group seeking to open its doors to black voters. Despite his forgiving philosophy, throughout his exemplary life Aris had suffered and fought against racial bigotry. In more ways than one, Aris Allen truly lived the American dream. Sadly, his life ended tragically. Diagnosed with terminal prostate cancer and unwilling to live without control of his independence and becoming a burden to his family, Aris Allen shot himself in the head with a shotgun. He was 80.

That tragic end doesn't diminish the accomplishments of this extraordinary man, and the community recognized it. Few citizens of Annapolis have a life-sized bust erected at the start of a major thoroughfare that bears their name as Aris does: "Aris T. Allen Boulevard."

Leonard Blackshear

Leonard Blackshear also has a pathway with his name on it, and it leads to a statue, but it is not of him. The statue is of author Alex Haley. The "Leonard A. Blackshear Walk" connects a story-wall along the Compromise Street side of the City Dock with a group of sculptures of the Kunta Kinte-Alex Haley memorial. The walk ends at the head of the dock, where Kunta Kinte would have been brought to be sold into slavery. The sit-by-me statues show Alex Haley reading to a multi-racial group of three children's sculptures. This memorial was largely due to the efforts of Leonard Blackshear, and a plaque there memorializes his role. It reads:

> *Leonard A. Blackshear Walk*
> *A Pathway to Reconciliation and Healing*
> *Founder and President of*
> *The Kunta Kinte-Alex Haley Foundation,*
> *His inspirational leadership created*
> *This Memorial Site*
> *And his tireless efforts encouraged racial healing and*
> *   promoted African-American History.*
> *1943-2006*

Leonard Blackshear had certainly felt the sting of discrimination himself, and I was witness to one such attempt to wound him. In the early 1970s, my wife, children and I lived in an all-white neighborhood outside of Annapolis called "Riva Woods." One day a neighbor came to see me to complain that a black family was planning to buy a house in our neighborhood, and he wanted me to help keep the family out. "They'll reduce the value of our houses," I remember him saying with a few racial slurs thrown in. I not only refused to help him, but said I would actively oppose any such attempt. It seemed to take the wind out of his bigoted sails. So,

Leonard Blackshear and his family moved into Riva Woods.

I made Leonard's acquaintance in the neighborhood and the community at large, where we were both active in various organizations. We bonded a bit over our degrees from the same school, The University of Maryland, his in physics, mine in journalism. I found Leonard to be exceptionally bright and eminently likeable. He certainly was successful in careers with the likes of IBM and his own telecommunications company, TeleSonic Inc., where he helped pioneer the early use of voice mail and adapted technology for the deaf and disabled.

But Leonard's true calling was as champion of African-American causes, having started on that path as a youth in New York City working with Malcolm X through the Harlem Youth Opportunities Forum. In Annapolis, he worked to promote more opportunities for minority businessmen, helped create the United Black Clergy group in Anne Arundel County, and promoted black and white reconciliation events.

But his greatest achievement was the Kinte-Haley foundation and, prior to his death from cancer in 2006, Leonard was honored with the Dream Keepers Award from a local civil rights coalition for continuing Martin Luther King, Jr.'s legacy.

His memory is present to the multitudes who trod the Leonard A. Blackshear Walk at the City Dock.

Zastrow Simms

Joseph "Zastrow" Simms also has a memorial with his name on it, appropriately on a community center in the Fourth Ward's Obery Court neighborhood. "Zastrow" Simms ended up a respected community activist and youth supporter, but he didn't' start out that way. He took a circuitous route to prominence in the community.

A standout athlete, "Zas," as he was known to most of us, played with us in some of those childhood sandlot games, and he became the best athlete at all-black Bates High School. His athletic prowess led to his nickname, taken from Robert "Zug" Zastrow, Navy's quarterback who led the "upset of the half-century" win over Army in 1950. An honor roll student, Zas even got football scholarship interests from black colleges. But the fun-loving, womanizing side of the handsome, sturdy young man got the better of him, as did the accompanying need for money. His way to get it—burglary—led to prison, from which, remarkably, he began his civic career.

It's a well-known local story, wonderfully depicted in the video "Pip & Zastrow, An American Friendship." But it bears a condensed retelling here, especially since I was among the Annapolitans who witnessed it, and it involved my boyhood friend and teammate, Pip Moyer.

But, let me first set up the story with a personal digression. On Thursday, April 4, 1968, Martin Luther King, Jr. was assassinated and as a result almost immediately riots and looting broke out in cities across the country, including nearby Baltimore; Cambridge, Maryland; and Washington, D.C. The day after the assassination, in mid-afternoon, I was walking back to the Kiplinger Building, where I was associate editor of its magazine *Changing Times*, after a long lunch at the National Press Club with an old Journalism College professor. As I sauntered down H Street, I noticed a jeweler hurriedly pulling down his safety gate to lock up his store. Finding this strange in mid-afternoon I asked him if everything was ok. He pointed behind me, exclaiming "Look!"

I turned to see smoke rising above the downtown buildings. Washington was on fire and rioters would not let firefighters near the infernos. Heading home immediately, I drove a long route to Annapolis via the beltway since my normal route would have taken me right through the riot-torn area. On the beltway I witnessed the strangest sight, a line of tanks heading in the other direction toward Washington. The White House had ordered the military occupation of Washington, D.C.

As I grappled with the traffic on the beltway (the usual 45 minute drive home took me four hours), I wondered fearfully if the fiery riots would be repeated in Annapolis. That's when Pip and Zastrow wrote the most heroic chapter of an American friendship.

I have already established Pip Moyer's basketball bona fides, but Zastrow had them, too. In fact the two became great friends through basketball, playing together on some all-star black teams. As far as I know, Pip was the only white player selected to play for the Falcons, a talented black team in Annapolis, which caused some consternation among his white friends and some relatives, especially when the team picture showed up in the newspaper showing Pip and the black men. But Pip's rapport with the black community, forged originally in his Eastport upbringing and nourished on the basketball court, would be critically important later, as a politician and in the dire times following Martin Luther King, Jr.'s assassination.

In 1965, with the overwhelming support of the black vote, Pip became the youngest Mayor ever elected in Annapolis. While old friends like me helped peripherally on Pip's campaign, it was black friends like Zastrow who really got the vote out. Meanwhile Zastrow was in and out of jail. In fact, he was in jail when his mother died, and Pip interceded with authorities to have Zastrow furloughed to attend her funeral. That effort presaged another critical furlough.

Black leaders and clergymen managed to keep the lid on most violence in Annapolis for a few days after King's death, but black youths, spurred on by outside rabble rousers, began to gather in the streets of Annapolis Harlem with the intention of destroying government buildings as an act of rebellion against authority. They actually marched to the City Dock with mayhem in mind. Into this maelstrom of black anger stepped the white mayor. With his "street cred," Pip was able to calm the young blacks with one-to-one talks, but he knew he needed more credibility, and he knew where to get it.

With the support of Governor Spiro Agnew, Pip called the Warden of the Maryland State Penitentiary in Baltimore, asking that Zastrow Simms be furloughed. The furlough was granted and Zastrow joined Pip walking the streets of Annapolis, counseling restraint and promising respite. To give the young blacks diversionary activities, Pip and Zas staged a band musical and dance at a Fourth Ward hall, and 800 kids showed up. While

Baltimore burned, Annapolis danced.

Zastrow Simms turned his life around. Granted a full pardon by the state, he went to work for the City's urban renewal program and was later named director of the Stanton Community Center in the Fourth Ward, featuring sports, arts and cultural events for all Annapolitans. Zas became famous for his shepherding hundreds of black kids free-of-charge to major sports events and Broadway plays, and generally improving their quality of life. Later in life, Zas was recognized as a pillar of the community, picking up a new nickname, "Godfather of Annapolis."

Aris Allen, Leonard Blackshear and Zastrow Sims are but three of the many African-American leaders who helped turn the tide of segregation in Annapolis. They overcame much since the terrible days of slavery and Dred Scott.

The statue of Marylander Roger Brooke Taney, in front of the State House, honors the fifth Chief Justice of the United States. Taney was also author of the infamous Dred Scott decision.

On my trip to the State House to revisit this playground of my youth, I reflected on racial paradox in the life of the Dred Scott decision-maker, Roger Brooke Taney, on whose statue I sat as a youngster. Roger Taney holds a distinguished place in Maryland and American history, having served as the fifth Chief Justice of the United States. A Maryland native, he distinguished himself as one of the state's best lawyers, having studied law and practiced in Annapolis. He went from being Attorney General of Maryland to acting U.S. Secretary of War to accepting President Andrew Jackson's nomination as Attorney General of the U.S. to Jackson's nominee for the Supreme Court.

Despite this distinguished career, Taney is most remembered for delivering the majority opinion in *Dred Scott vs. Sandford* (1857) that ruled that African Americans, having been considered inferior at the time the Constitution was drafted, were not part of the community of citizens covered by it, and, therefore, could not be considered citizens of the United States.

Thus, Taney's court ruled that Dred Scott, born into slavery, could not sue in court for his freedom even though his master had taken him to live in free territories. Taney infamously wrote of blacks:

> *They had for more than a century before been regarded as beings of an inferior order, and altogether unfit to associate with the white race, either in social or political relations, and so far unfit that they had no rights which the white man was bound to respect.*

Lincoln in Annapolis

This decision, (considered to have indirectly hastened the Civil War) caused condemnation by many, especially Abraham Lincoln.

Annapolis played a small part in President Lincoln's efforts to end the Civil War. In February of 1865, just a few months before the war ended, encouraged by General Ulysses Grant, Lincoln travelled to Fort Monroe, a union-held fortress at Hampton Roads, Virginia, to meet with Confederate peace commissioners to explore the remote possibility of a cease fire to end the horrendous killing of war combatants.

Since ice blocked the ports near Washington, Lincoln travelled to Annapolis by rail, arriving at the corner of Calvert and West Streets, near where that rail station still operated in my youth carrying the Midshipmen to the Army-Navy game. Lincoln, accompanied only by a servant, bodyguard and a Union Army officer, Captain Gardner Blodgett, walked through town, on a less than one mile trip to a deep water wharf at the Naval Academy. Lincoln certainly passed in sight of the State House, where the Maryland Senate was considering ratification of the Thirteenth Amendment, abolishing slavery in the U.S. Boarding a steamboat, Lincoln's party headed out the Severn River and down the Chesapeake Bay to Fort Monroe, where the Confederate Commissioners awaited. Lincoln's insistence that nothing could be negotiated unless the commissioners first agreed to the dissolutions of the Confederate Government, effectively ended the negotiations.

Two days after he arrived, Lincoln returned up the Bay to Annapolis and took a special train back to Washington. Lincoln's trip is fully explored in a fascinating short book *Lincoln in Annapolis: February 1865*, by Rockford E. Toews and published by the Maryland State Archives.

Toews does an artful job of picturing Lincoln's walk through Annapolis:

> *Traffic along the streets and rail line leading into the Naval Academy would have almost certainly have been congested by the additional pressure put on the military port by the closure of surrounding ports by ice. Wagons, carts, troops, animals—all would have made it difficult for Lincoln to travel through Annapolis by carriage, and the rail line probably could not have been cleared either, given the short notice of his arrival.*
>
> *Perhaps Lincoln, anticipating a long boat ride and fearing his usual seasickness, wished to get some fresh air. Or maybe he wanted to stretch his long legs after the railroad ride from Washington. The railroad extension laid in 1861 to connect the depot to the waterfront along the Naval Academy becomes important to the story of Lincoln in Annapolis because it may well be that Blodgett walked Lincoln along this route as they made their way to the wharf. The city's unpaved streets were almost certainly mud, and it is probably that the best walking would have followed the rail line, which led directly where they wanted to go.*

Lincoln, of course, never returned to Annapolis. Two months

after his trip to Hampton Roads, he was assassinated.

While the Thirteenth Amendment was not ratified by the states until December of 1865, five months after Lincoln died, Maryland abolished slavery more than a year earlier, on October 12, 1864. Ironically, on that same day, Roger Brooke Taney passed away.

A Walk from Intolerance to Tolerance

Roger Taney is a paradoxical figure. The first paradox: Taney considered slavery an evil and freed his own slaves when he inherited them and provided pensions for those too old to work. And once, when defending a Methodist minister indicted for inciting slave insurrections, Taney condemned slavery as "a blot on our national character."

Another paradox: Taney personally administered the oath of office to one of his harshest critics, President Abraham Lincoln.

While historians condemn Taney for his Dred Scott opinion, they generally agree it is the one blot on an otherwise distinguished career on the Supreme Court, where he served as Chief Justice for 28 years.

On that trip to the State House to revisit this playground of my childhood, touring the Capitol with family friend and Speaker of the Maryland House of Delegates Michael Busch, Mike put another paradox in what might be called a statuesque perspective. Mike and I stood beside the Old Senate Chamber, where Washington resigned his commission, and looked out the front window at the statue of Roger Brooke Taney. Mike commented about how far we had come in the 150 plus years since Taney delivered his Dred Scott opinion. "You only have to walk from the front of the State House to the back where you can look out on another statue of a Maryland-born Supreme Court Justice, Thurgood Marshall, to understand how far we have come in the march towards civil rights," Mike explained.

There, behind the State House, on what's called "Lawyer's Mall," is the imposing statue of Thurgood Marshall, who argued many a civil rights case before the Supreme Court before joining its ranks in 1967. One of his most important victories, as counsel for NAACP, was in *Brown vs. Board of Education*, which overturned the doctrine of separate but equal schools and, effectively, began the dismantling of all segregation laws.

Marshall's statue appropriately stands before the statues of three school-aged children in rapt attention to his soundless but prophetic arguments for racial justice and in sharp contrast to Roger Taney's *Dred Scott* opinion. A walk from the front of Maryland's State House to the rear mall is like walking from intolerance to tolerance.

On Lawyer's Mall behind the State House, stands a statue honoring native Marylander Thurgood Marshall, who successfully argued many civil rights cases at the Supreme Court before joining its ranks in 1967.

When Barack Obama was elected the first black President, it seemed to still the remnants of discrimination so prevalent for so long after Kunta Kinte's arrival in Annapolis and the flawed legal arguments of the Dred Scott decision. Not quite still, of course, but I believe we're on our way to a color blind country, though it still may take generations.

In a creative writing course in college, I wrote a play titled "Three Acts in Tan." The premise of the play was that in ten generations from the 1950s, the color divide in America could disappear through intermingling of the races, producing a homogeneous race of tan people. The only problem was that some white babies still were also born, and they became the outcasts.

My premise may not have been too far out, though somewhat simplistic. Intermarriage of races is so much more prevalent now, and scientists studying DNA have shown that we are all a mixture of races, ethnicities and geographic origins. Since all are such a mixture, perhaps someday no one will be an outcast.

CHAPTER TWENTY

THREE CENTURIES LATER

On May 21, 1949, a date picked to start celebrating the 300th anniversary of Annapolis' settlement, I became a Susquehannock Indian, complete with a faux buckskin outfit and a massive feather headdress. For Annapolis' Tercentenary celebration, I had been chosen to represent one of the Severn River area's first inhabitants. *Evening Capital* and Associated Press photos of the event show me, a fresh-faced high school freshman, smiling brightly below billowing feathers at Patricia Anne West, who was chosen to preside over the pageant as England's Queen Anne, the City's namesake.

Following the May 21 Saturday evening's start of the celebration, Monday's *Evening Capital* colorfully described the event:

> *The blaze of trumpets, a swirling mass of red, white and blue flags, horses prancing, a white coach bearing the Princess Anne, a sudden still picture of the brilliant mass of figures and color—so the story of Annapolis began to unfold in the City's Tercentenary Pageant 'Song of the Severn.'*

The pageant celebrated the history of Annapolis, featuring white wigged actors as Washington, Lafayette, et al; 19th century midshipmen in straw hats; a train running through downtown Annapolis; and us Susquehannocks signing a treaty with the settlers under a fake "Liberty Tree," representing the massive old poplar then still standing on St. Johns' campus.

This all took place on Annapolis High School's hardscrabble athletic field, on a huge stage erected where, just days before, I had been practicing lacrosse with our high school team. So I went from Indian game to Indian actor. What I recall most from the pageant was the deluge that drove us inside that first night, creating drooping headdress feathers, and the pageant parade that took us down West Street and Main Street around the dock to King

George Street and past a reviewing stand on the St. Johns' campus along College Avenue. I was quite proud and happy waving to friends and neighbors along the way, none of us realizing that this celebration of the past portended the end of an era. Nineteen forty-nine was a watershed year.

As 1950 dawned in Annapolis, fear was everywhere. To steal an expression from professional football of that era, we faced "A Fearsome Foursome." They were McCarthyism, the Cold War, the Korean War and nuclear bombs. Given the destructive nature of the latter two, a more apt comparison might be to "The Four Horsemen of the Apocalypse."

While the first two didn't have much direct impact on us high school teenagers, the second two were omnipresent in our daily lives.

As the summer between my sophomore and junior year in high school began, news came that communist North Korea had invaded South Korea. While the conflict began as a civil war, it escalated into a battle between the U.S. and its allies and North Korea and its allies, China and Russia. When the United Nations force, led by the U.S., joined the battle, the North Korean Army collapsed, but then China, with its hundreds of thousands of soldiers, entered the fray, and a bloody stalemate ensued for two more years. By the time an armistice was signed in July of 1953, more than 33,000 American soldiers died and about 100,000 were wounded.

At Annapolis High School, the war really came into the classroom in 1951 when seven of our male classmates graduated a year early by volunteering to fight in Korea. My thoughts at the time were quite parochial, thinking we had lost our best pitcher, David Burtis, for the 1952 baseball season, and I would not see my friend Ben Sarles that summer on Spa Creek, where his family owned the oldest boat yard in the City.

I didn't worry about going to war because Annapolis High had a two-track curriculum, the A (for academic) Track and the C (for commercial) Track. The C Track guys would face the draft when they graduated. The A Track boys, headed for college, would be deferred from the draft. I was in the A Track.

A Digression

In 1958, newly married and working at the *Baltimore News Post*, I received my delayed draft notice to report to Fort Jackson, South Carolina. So, Carlotta and I gave up our jobs, cancelled our apartment lease, and prepared to move south. Since I had remained in the Reserves since I was 18, I paid a visit to the draft board office on Church Circle to see if that Reserve service would enhance my military pay.

"What reserve?" The draft board secretary asked.

"Now I'm in the Standby Reserves," I answered.

She got a funny look on her face. "General H was just here this week; and he told us we were no longer drafting standby reservists," she said.

Incredulous, I anxiously responded, "But I've already been drafted!"

"Talk to the general," she said.

"Where is he?" I asked, grasping at hope.

"In the Fifth Regiment Armory in Baltimore."

A thought popped into my head. My City Editor, Eddie Ballard, knew everyone of importance in Baltimore. I called Eddie immediately.

"Do you know General H?" I asked.

"Sure do, kid," Eddie replied.

So I explained the situation. He said he'd call me back, and in less than an hour he did.

"General H wants to see you," Eddie said, "Get your butt up to the armory."

My butt was in the car right away, and I flew from Annapolis to Baltimore in about 35 minutes. At the armory, I was ushered into General H's office.

Believe it or not, he took one look at me and said something like: "You look like a good kid. You don't have to go to Fort Jackson. I'll send the paperwork to your draft board."

What jubilation I felt. We got back our jobs and apartment; and life went on as usual, all because of a lucky happenstance. Yet, there was another lesson learned: Don't underestimate the power of the press.

The Korean War had a fearsome, unexpected consequence; it increased efforts in the United States to develop a weapon even more deadly than the atomic bomb. Since the Russians had unexpectedly developed their atomic bomb after World War II, some U.S. physicists, generals and politicians believed we needed to one-up the Soviets in destructive power. The "H-Bomb," a nickname derived from "Hydrogen Bomb," a thermonuclear device, was first exploded in 1952. It was more than 450 times more powerful than the atomic bomb dropped on Nagasaki during World War II.

The atomic bomb could wipe out cities. The H-Bomb could wipe out mankind. It didn't take long—1953—for the Russians to develop an H-Bomb so the Cold War threat of nuclear attack troubled Americans, and that concern trickled down to us high schoolers.

Those were the "duck and cover" days at Annapolis High, as if covering your head with your hands in the school hallway would protect you from a nuclear explosion. But it was just a reflection of the national angst about the possibility of nuclear wars. Some Americans even built bomb shelters in their backyard; others searched for places of protection from radiation fall out. My folks and I decided the apartment cellar would be the safest place, but we made no preparations beyond that decision—no canned goods, drinking water or other emergency supplies. Without them, the cellar would have been as much help as "duck and cover."

Ultimately, the nuclear stalemate and a growing economy wiped away our fears. With memories of the Great Depression receding and World War II behind us, times were good. My dad's job at the Academy was secure, and mom easily found work as a bank teller, bringing in a second income that allowed for some consumer comforts—a car to drive to Baltimore occasionally and our first TV set. Main Street stores were busy, as consumerism grew throughout the country.

While the 1950s were good to my family, we couldn't get away from the third floor apartment, where Mr. Elliott kept the rent low and, with his mechanical skills, dad took care of the furnace in the cellar as part of the deal. Around that time, a small, row house on Conduit Street came up for sale for $5,000, and my mom really wanted it, but we just couldn't swing it financially.

Changed but Unchanged

Annapolis changed dramatically in 1950. On one day—May 23—voters in neighborhoods surrounding the City increased its size sevenfold and doubled the population. After years of haggling, citizens approved annexation of Eastport, Germantown-

Homewood, West Annapolis and Parole, increasing the City's area from the three quarters of a mile, bounded by Spa and College Creeks, to encompass five and a half square miles and raising the population from 10,000 to 20,000. So the kids that were neighborhood sports adversaries of my youth—such as the "Eastport Bonecrushers"—were now Annapolitans, though they didn't appreciate it. Once an Eastporter (before annexation) always an Eastporter.

A bit earlier in 1950—February 5 to be exact—the bouncy, swaying train rides I took to Baltimore as a braces-wearing youngster ended for all travelers when passenger service to the Bladen Street station ended. Thereafter you had to drive or take the bus. Transportation took an evolutionary step forward in 1952, the year I graduated from High School, with the opening of the first span of the Chesapeake Bay Bridge, which ended the bay's ferry service.

My world changed dramatically, as well, with my June, 1952 graduation. My class graduated from the stage of the auditorium where I had been so many times, from the first day at Annapolis High, through many assemblies, plays and music classes. I even spent some time there as the school band bass drummer in front of the assembled students. My first public attention for writing happened there when an assembly was read my poem "Four Years." While I don't remember much about our graduation, I'll never forget—nor will most of my classmates—the anonymous maxim in bas-relief above the stage:

> "The measure of a man is the depth of his convictions, the breadth of his interests, and the height of his ideals."

Hopefully, those words helped guide us through life after high school.

At our high school class graduation dinner, we read prophesies for each graduate. The prophecy for school newspaper writers Gregg Magruder and Ralph Crosby: "Gregg and Ralph will become award-winning journalists!" Gregg became a banker. At the class 10th Anniversary celebration, I received a small trophy for "Prophecy Most Closely Fulfilled."

Though I went off to college that fall, I continued to live at 183 on weekends and in the summer. So, I kept an eye on Main Street as its transformation continued. That transformation was symbolized by a single event—the moving of the Carroll Barrister house from

Main Street to the St. John's College campus.

Our longtime neighbor Mary Ella Davis died on February 21, 1953, at age 81. Until she went to a convalescent home toward the end of her life, Miss Davis lived in the historic house her mother had bought in 1873. She was buried with a spray of the house's ancient boxwood in her hand. That was the boxwood through which I always ran my fingers as I turned onto Conduit Street from Main Street. Her executors, relatives including her nephew — my friendly landlord — Arthur Elliott, disposed of her property, including the beloved boxwood hedges, which were older than the Revolution. A *Baltimore Sun* classified ad of the time noted "For Sale. Eleven boxwood bushes over 200 years old in the yards of the house corner of Main and Conduit Streets." They also auctioned off the family's antique furniture and "classical books."

I don't know who bought the boxwoods or the books, but the property itself was purchased by local clothing store owner and entrepreneur, Joe Greenfield.

Joe Greenfield's *Peerless Clothing* was a Main Street institution. Joe was something of local institution himself, known for his sporty, outgoing style. I knew Joe tangentially, being friendly with some of his younger family members and working in his store during college Christmas vacation in 1954. Walking to work at Peerless down Main Street that Christmas time, I'd pass the steps of the Carroll Barrister house where my buddies and I often gathered, and the boxwood bushes on the corner never thinking they would soon disappear along with the tangled garden where I picked pears, apples and grapes.

Known at the time as the "Carroll Davis House," in honor of the Davis family owners, it would be turned to commercial use by Joe Greenfield. To have an 18th Century town house sitting in the middle of the City's commercial district was something of an anomaly. But to demolish this historic and architectural gem, as Joe Greenfield planned, would have been sinful. Enter a recently formed group of preservationists called "Historic Annapolis," led by the indomitable Anne St. Clair Wright. Formed in 1952, this preservation group had its eye on the destined-for-commerce Carroll Barrister House property from the start. Saving the house was a cause to rally around, and the group's success in preserving the house gave it strength.

Joe Greenfield deeded the house to Historic Annapolis, which raised $20,000 to move it, and St. John's College agreed to provide a campus site for it. Over two days, October 3 and 4, 1955, as my mom watched from the third floor window of 183, the old house was cut in two fairly equal portions, lifted off its foundation and slowly wheeled up Main Street. *The Evening Capital* of the day gave a graphic reporting of the event:

Our apartment's neighbor, the Carroll Barrister House, torn from its centuries-old location in 1955, moves up Main Street toward its new location at St. John's College. (Courtesy of M.E. Warren Photography, LLC)

After more than two centuries of existence, the old house proved to be the indomitable veteran it is. It was stubborn and slow but showed no signs of collapsing.

Hundreds of persons gathered to watch the move — probably the most spectacular ever staged in Annapolis. Some were there early, arriving shortly after 5:30 A.M. when men from the power company first began removing lines to permit the exit of the house, still shrouded in fog, onto the street.

LIKE AN OLD LADY sorry to leave her home, the

house moved unwillingly, and by 9 A.M. was well behind
a schedule which called for her to be at Church Circle at
that time.

The Main Street end of the house managed to go
over an improvised wooden runway from the curbing
to the street only by 8:20 A.M., crushing the edge of the
sidewalk as it moved.

It was attached by cable to two heavy trucks, former
marine equipment weighted down by cinderblock and a
tractor. They were anchored fast to the street and the
house was wrenched, or pulled toward it.

At 6:50 A.M. the first move was made, and the 125-
ton house inched forward. For over three hours afterwards
the four workmen on the job worked tediously to move the
house several feet at a time.

Backed out first, the house by 10:15 A.M. had finally
maneuvered the 45 degree angle necessary to permit it
to go up Main Street. At 11:40 A.M. it was in front of
Woolworth's.

From there it was to go up Main Street to Church
Circle, to College Avenue, King George Street, and St.
John's College, where it will be erected between the
gymnasium and the boxwood garden.

The old house rests gently on the St. John's campus where it
was deposited in 1955, since that day serving as administrative
offices for the college. It was the first great preservation victory
for Historic Annapolis and St. Clair Wright. There would be
many more, including restoring William Paca's illustrious house
and gardens on Prince George Street; the Shiplap House, a small
home, sawmill and tavern built in 1715, and the Victualling House,
a warehouse across from City Dock at 77 Main Street, which had
stored supplies for the Continental Army.

A navy daughter and navy wife, St. Clair Wright had ties to
Annapolis long before she settled in the City and became its
architectural protector. Both sweet and feisty, Mrs. Wright, as I
always called her, could turn on the charm when she wanted
support, which I gave her in my days as President of the Annapolis
Chamber of Commerce. But she turned steely when I asked
her if the Chamber could use the Victualling House as a tourist
information center. "Ralph," she said, "I believe you're trying to
steal our building." Needless to say, the Chamber didn't get to use

the building, but my support for Mrs. Wright never flagged. She had done too much for the city—transforming its appearance and buoying the economy—for me to hold a grudge. And, after all, Historic Annapolis had use of this state-owned building. It was Mrs. Wright who most succinctly described the city, in a foreword to a book of photos, *Annapolis*, by photographer Kevin Fleming:

> *Annapolis is a museum without walls, a living landmark*
> *three centuries in the making. It has rightly been called*
> *'the most individual small town in the entire country.'*

The Carroll Barrister property, as mentioned earlier, became a Burger King in 1957, an early entry in what I call the "restauranting" of Annapolis. Historic Annapolis' efforts were so successful that more and more people wanted to visit Annapolis. The Naval Academy and the waterfront had always brought tourists to town, but now they came in waves to walk the Ancient City. And these tourists had to eat.

Restauranting of Annapolis

Eventually, one after another, my boyhood haunts and Annapolis landmarks turned into restaurants. Much to my chagrin, included were my two favorite youthful hideaways. Reynolds' Tavern reverted to one of its original purposes, turning from library to tavern, and the pool room on Main Street eventually traded the pool tables for dining tables.

Probably the most significant restaurant opening occurred in 1960, when George Phillips, a Baltimorean fresh out of managing a Marriott Hot Shoppe, came to town and opened a small, 90-seat eatery he named The Harbour House. It was on the harbor, separated from the City Dock by a sprawling, metered parking lot—one of George's reasons for selecting that location. George recognized the latent value of tourism and the dock location with its available parking.

Locals questioned George's sanity, opening a restaurant in Hell Point and charging a dollar for a hamburger when you could buy a bag of burgers for a buck at the Little Tavern. But crab cakes, seafood and steaks were George's forte and soon locals and tourists were flocking to The Harbour House, and within a few years, George's success had expanded his restaurant to 350 seats. Other entrepreneurs soon saw the dock area as a restauranteurs paradise.

The Hardestys turned Mandris' back into Middleton Tavern; the Hyatts, my friends Lou and his brother Mel, remade their Market Space bar into an upper scale Dockside Restaurant; and pilot Mike Ashford opened a restaurant/bar where the old black pool room had been on Dock Street and named it after his grandmother McGarvey. Jenkins' stationery store, next to 183 Main, became a French restaurant.

I shouldn't complain about the restauranting of Annapolis, for it is what allowed me to flex my entrepreneurial muscles. George Phillips was a neighbor who became a close friend. He is the one who ended my journalism career. At the height of his success, George asked me to join him in business as the chief marketer and developer of new business, of which I would receive a "piece of the action." That opportunity allowed me to work in my home town, where my children were growing up, and afforded me the chance to start my own, little advertising/public relations agency. Eventually the agency tail wagged the other businesses' dog, and it became my full-time, joyful venture, much assisted by my "piece of the action" attained through George Phillips' largesse.

"Sailing Capital of the World"

Restaurants weren't the only things that changed the City Dock. By the 1950s, the Chesapeake Bay became as much a pleasure boating mecca as a fishing center. Where I rowed my castaway row boat on Spa Creek, sleek sailboats and massive yachts, some measuring more than 200 feet, plied the waters. Some of the smaller pleasure craft owners liked to show off their boats in the City Dock, which then took on the nickname, "Ego Alley." The famous Annapolis-Newport race, which started in the late 1940s, spawned other Annapolis-based races and regattas, such as the Annapolis-Bermuda race, and the racing bug spread throughout the City, where there is a race almost every night in spring and summer. The Annapolis Yacht Club even hosts a "Frostbite" race on winter Sundays, where sailors brave the freezing weather to compete for glory but no gain except an after-race party.

All this pleasure boating activity led to development of the annual U.S. Sailboat and Powerboat in-the-water Boat Shows with sailboats and yachts filling the City Dock and the parking lot in front of what was The Harbour House Restaurant. The Boat Shows, which attract 100,000 people to the City Dock in October each year, are one measure of Annapolis' boating dominance.

Plus, of course, the Naval Academy has one of the nation's most active sailing programs, thanks in part to my friend Bob McNitt. All of this activity has caused tiny Annapolis to earn the sobriquet the "Sailing Capital of America." Both Naval Academy and City officials have labeled it the "Sailing Capital of the World," but that seems a bit grandiose.

The boating activity helped create another dramatic change in the waterfront. At my boyhood swimming holes on Spa Creek and Horn Point, the shoreline is filled with expensive condominiums where boatyards used to stand beside pristine coves and woods, and hundreds of sailboat masts line the piers in front of these condos.

Despite its evolution from broad colonial harbor to narrow "Ego Alley," the City Dock has acted as the fulcrum of Annapolis' fortunes. It was so in my youth. It is so now, still the base support for Main Street. If you stood at the head of the dock behind the statue of Alex Haley, as I did these many decades after the 1950s, you'd be reminded of the old proverb "The more things change, the more they stay the same." Sure, there are old things missing from Main Street, including two of my favorites, the Carroll Barrister House and the Republic Theater. The small grocery stores and the five- and ten-cent stores are all gone, and so are the milliners and dry goods shops.

Beacons: Past, Present and Future

But the City's four dominant spires still reach their way on high. The Naval Academy Chapel dome offers a beacon for the new, young, midshipmen, and maybe an astronaut or even a future president worships there. Hopefully it has a better repair platform than the rope seat my dad used.

If you sailed on the Severn today, past Greenbury Point, you'd see three of the former 19 radio towers still standing, tall sentries over location of the historic Providence settlement, now mostly submerged by the river.

The State House dome looks down on the City, covering the legislature in its annual meetings as it has for 200-plus years and protecting "the most historic room in America" where Washington resigned his military commission, a room restored in 2015 to look like it did 230 plus years ago. St. Anne's Church's clock tower bells continue to serenade its citizens from its Church Circle perch, and St. Mary's Church steeple, as always, calls its parishioners to worship, including my grandchildren who attend the high school next door.

On Main Street, as recently as 2008 named "one of the great streets in America," the store names have changed, but most of the store fronts remain as I remember them from my boyhood; and working class families still live in the apartments above the stores.

And 183 Main Street is still there, with a storefront on the ground floor and two apartments above. Perhaps today a young boy bounds up those two floors of steps thinking he is Superman and looks out the front windows onto Main Street, dreaming about what he'll do when he grows up.

I dreamed about being a writer.

EPILOGUE

Sweet Memories

As I recalled my youthful days in Annapolis, it inevitably led to my first great adventure away from home and the end of childhood — college. My mom drove me the 25 miles to College Park, home of the University of Maryland that Fall of 1952. We gave a ride to my friend Pip Moyer, later mayor of Annapolis, who was going to Maryland on a basketball scholarship, though he would leave in our freshman year for Baltimore University, where he became a star player.

I made two new friends that summer between high school and college. I knew neither one before the summer of 1952 when we bonded over our common entry to the university. Fred Wiedenbauer's father was a former World War II German Army Officer who had gotten a job as a maintenance man at St. Mary's High School, and Fred went to school there, so we never met in high school. While Frank Huckel's mother was from Annapolis, his father was a naval officer who moved from one station to another. They had come to Annapolis to live that summer. Through mutual friends who haunted our Main Street hangouts, the three of us discovered we were off to Maryland, and we began palling around together. That friendship continued once we got to College Park, playing together on the same intramural football and basketball teams, joining an independent students' club, and rooming together the first semester of our junior year before they both left college.

Frank went off to be a language translator for the National Security Agency, I believe, and I eventually lost track of him. Fred became a Navy pilot, and we remained close though a distance apart until his untimely death from lung cancer in the 1970s. Fred, a tall, strapping, good natured guy would often visit my wife and me in Annapolis, and I'll never forget his last visit and the throat-choking pain I felt as he drove away from my house. I knew it was the last time I would see him, and it was. He died shortly thereafter, and I never knew when and where his funeral occurred or where he was buried. He had a brother in Boston, and I assume he was buried there. Thus the memories of Fred are bittersweet.

The Three Musketeers off to college. Here I'm flanked by my pals Frank Huckel (left) and Fred Wiedenbauer (right), c. 1953.

When you are mining your memory bank, as I was doing for this memoir, you come up with some cherished nuggets. As it has for some writers more talented than I, such nuggets can create a stream of consciousness that brings forth more hidden memories.

The stream of consciousness that brought Fred and Frank back to memory happened while I was writing this book's chapter "Hi-Yo Silver! Away!" and recalling the music of my youth, headlined by Bing Crosby. In those days, I was often teased, "Can you sing like Bing?" Heck, I could hardly carry a tune. But writing about it brought to mind my experience singing on the street corner.

In the 1950s, movies about teens often had them singing in harmony on the streets. While "harmony" isn't the right word for it, I did the same with Fred and Frank on Main Street.

We'd move from the Wardroom to the pool room to LaRosa's for pizza, and sing our way down Main Street.

The one song we did well was an old Civil War folk song called "Poor Old Slave." Don't ask me how we heard of it, but the fun was in adding repetitious words or syllables to the main words. The basic words, as we sang them, were:

> *The poor old slave has gone to rest,*
> *At last we know he's free.*
> *His bones, they lie, disturb that not.*
> *Way down in Tennessee.*

The next stanza would add some words:

The poor poor old slave slave has gone gone to rest rest
At last we know he's free, oh free free,
His bones, bones, they lie, lie, disturb, turb them not, not
Way down, down in Tenn-, Tennessee, see.

The song would keep growing in complication until we got to
something like:

The piggity-pag poor old sliggity slag slave has jigity-gag gone to
riggity-rag rest.
We kniggity-knag know that higgity-hag he is friggity-fag free,
oh free free.
His biggity-bag bones, they liggity-lag lie, distiggity-turb them,
niggity-nag not
Way diggity-dag down in tiggity-tag Tennessee—o—see—see.

We even had nicknames for our trio. Frank at five foot nine
or so was "little one," I was "middle-sized one" at six feet, and at
six foot two, Fred was "big one." Fred played an important role
in my life in those college years, no role more important than on
January 1, 1955, when Fred's date got me that blind date for a party
at Carvel Hall with the 17-year-old, raven-haired beauty, Carlotta,
who became my wife in June of 1958. As noted earlier, I made that
blind date call to Carlotta from Fred's apartment on Shipwright
Street which, in a strange coincidence, was where Carlotta lived
when I proposed to her. When taking our children to and from
nearby St. Mary's Schools, we would often ride on Shipwright
Street past that apartment, bringing back memories of our youthful
romance.

That's the wonderful thing about living your life in one small
town. Memories are freshly reborn often. I experience that every
time I drive or walk on Main Street. I can still see Fred and Frank
singing down Main Street with me. I often look up at the third
floor front room windows of 183, and I'm transported back to my
childhood and the Carroll Barrister gardens, the Republic Theater,
Green Street School, and the many playgrounds and work places of
growing up in America's Ancient City.

Every time I walk past 183 Main Street, I touch the brick sides
of the front steps, where we often sat, in fond remembrance of my
mom and dad.

When I was a freshman in college, I wrote a rather juvenile
poem to express to my parents how I felt about them and sent it to

them in a letter. The poem:

Two little words, mom and dad,
They mean all the world to me.
They raised me, they loved me
Through sickness and health.
They showered me with gifts
Even though they lacked wealth.
But I guess you don't need money
When that thing called love is free.
Love, that's what we have,
Mom and dad—and me.

Long after my parents had passed on, I found a copy of that poem among some old papers, rewritten in my mother's hand and lovingly preserved.

It was in a fireproof metal strongbox made by my dad, along with a five and ten cent store broach with the word "mother" in its center surrounded by multicolored stones. I gave the broach to mom on Mother's Day when I was seven or eight and told her the stones were diamonds and rubies. Although some of the stones had fallen out, she kept it among her treasures.

Sweet memories.

ACKNOWLEDGEMENTS

While such memoirs as this one chronicle the author's experiences and observations, no one writes such a book alone. It takes a lot of help.

In my case, I first want to acknowledge the help from Annapolis' premiere historian, the writer Jane McWilliams, for her invaluable editorial and historical guidance.

Thanks to the staffs of the Maryland Hall of Records, the state law library, the Annapolis Public Library, and the Naval Academy's Nimitz Library for leading me to the proper sources in my research. I'm especially grateful for the individual attention of Maria Day at the Maryland Archives. Thanks, also, to my son-in-law, David Butler, for his professional photographic help.

My gratitude to my Crosby Marketing colleague Claudia Eaton, one of the few who can decipher my hen scratchings, for turning my disorderly yellow pad pages into a manuscript.

Several old friends were helpful, such as Lou Hyatt, Les Trott and John Henneberger, whose tales of the Annapolis of our youth inspired me, and Mike Busch, Maryland's Speaker of the House, for his State House tours and stories. A tip of my literary hat to my longtime (from college) pal Hal Burdett, whose bookish conversations helped keep my writing gene alive.

Kudos to founder and editorial director of Anaphora Literary Press Anna Faktorovich for shepherding my book through the publishing process.

One more kiss to my son Ray and my daughters, Laura and Belinda, professional communicators all, for their hands-on guidance and support. And my undying gratitude to the love of my life, my wife Carlotta, without whose support this memoir would not have such a happy ending.

—Ralph Crosby
Annapolis, Maryland
Summer, 2016

SELECTED BIBLIOGRAPHY

Anderson, Elizabeth B. *Annapolis, A Walk Through History*. Centreville, Maryland: Tidewater Publishers, 1984.

Anderson, Lars. *The All Americans*. New York, N.Y.: St. Martin's Press, 2004.

Banning, Kendall (Revised by A. Stuart Pitt). *Annapolis Today*. New York: Funk and Wagnalls Company, 1938. Sixth Edition, 1968.

Barnes, Robert. *Colonial Families of Anne Arundel County, Maryland*. Westminster, Maryland: Family Living Publications, 1996.

Brashears, Dave. *Riding The Honeysuckle Horse: Growing Up in Eastport and Annapolis in the Forties and Early Fifties*. Annapolis: 2005.

Brown, Ford K. *The Annapolitan Library at St. John's College*. Annapolis. St. John's College, Annapolis, Maryland.

Brown, Philip L. *The Other Annapolis 1900-1950*. Annapolis, Maryland: The Annapolis Publishing Company, 1994.

Burdett, Harold N. *Yesteryear in Annapolis*, Centreville, Maryland: Tidewater Publishers, 1974.

Churchill, Winston. *Richard Carvel*. London, England: The Macmillan Company, 1899.

Delaplaine, Edward S. *Francis Scott Key: Life and Times*. A 2011 Facsimile Reprint by Heritage Books. Westminster, Maryland, 2011. Original published by Biography Press in 1937.

D'Este, Carlo. *Fatal Decision, Anzio and the Battle for Rome*. New York, N.Y.: Harper Collins, 1991.

Doyle, Ginger. *Annapolis Vignettes*. Centreville, Maryland: Tidewater Publishers, 2005.

Doyle, Ginger. *Gone To Market. The Annapolis Market House, 1698-2005*. Published by the City of Annapolis, Maryland, 2005.

Doyle, Ginger. *Over the Bridge, A History of Eastport at Annapolis*. Annapolis, Maryland: Annapolis Maritime Museum, 2008.

Fleming, Kevin. *Annapolis, the Spirit of the Chesapeake Bay*. Annapolis, Maryland: Portfolio Press, 1988.

Foster, Linda and Roger Miller. *United States Naval Academy*. Baltimore, Maryland: Image Publishing, 2001.

Fradin, Dennis Brindell. *The Signers, the 56 Stories Behind the Declaration of Independence*. New York, N.Y.: Walker & Company, 2002.

Good, Jane E. *High School Heroes, A Century of Education and Football at Annapolis High School 1896-2003*. Bowie, Maryland: Heritage Books, Inc., 2004.

Halberstam, David. *The Fifties*. New York: Villard Books, 1993.

Haley, Alex. *Roots*. New York, N.Y.: Vanguard Books, 1974.

Jackson, Elmer M. Jr. *Annapolis, Three Centuries of Glamour*. Annapolis,

Maryland: The Capital-Gazette Press, 1936.

Jensen, Ann. *The World Turned Upside Down: Children of 1776*. Centreville, Maryland: Tidewater Publishers, 2001.

Kaledin, Eugenia. *Daily Life in the United States 1940-1959—Shifting Worlds*. Westport, Connecticut: Greenwood Press, 2000.

Kyvig, David E. *Daily Life in the United States, 1920-1940, How Americans Lived Through the "Roaring Twenties" and the Great Depression*. Chicago, Illinois: Ivan R. Dee, Publisher, 2002.

Lossing, B.J. *Lives of the Signers of the Declaration of Independence*. Originally published in 1848. Texas: WallBuilders Press Reprint, 1995.

May, Jude Thomas. *Achieving the American Dream, The Life of the Honorable Aris T. Allen, M.D.* Baltimore, Maryland: Gateway Press, Inc., 1990.

McDermott, Scott. *Charles Carroll of Carrollton: Faithful Revolutionary*. New York: Sceptor, 2002.

McIntyre, Robert. *Annapolis, Maryland Families*. Baltimore: Gateway Press, 1979.

McWilliams, Jane Wilson. *Annapolis, City on the Severn*. Baltimore, Maryland: The Johns Hopkins University Press, 2011.

Middleton, Arthur Pierce. *Annapolis on the Chesapeake*. Greensborough, North Carolina: Legacy Publications, 1988.

Miller, Marcia M. and Orlando Ridout V. *Architecture in Annapolis, A Field Guide*. Crownsville, Maryland: Maryland Historical Trust, 1998.

Miller, Roger and Ginny Pearce. *Annapolis, Sailing Capital of Maryland*. Baltimore, Maryland: Image Publishing, 2009.

Morris, R. Rebecca. *A Low, Dirty Place, The Parole Camps of Annapolis, Md. 1862-1865*. Linthicum, Maryland: Ann Arrundell Historical Society, 2012.

Murphy, Emily A. *"A Complete & Generous Education," 300 years of Liberal Arts, St. John's College, Annapolis*. Annapolis, Maryland: St. John's College Press, 1996.

Norris, Walter B. *Annapolis, Its Colonial & Naval History*. New York, N.Y.: Thomas Y. Crowell Company, 1925.

Papenfuse, Edward C. *In Pursuit of Profit. The Annapolis Merchants in the Era of the American Revolution 1763-1805*. Baltimore: Johns Hopkins University Press, 1975.

Ridgely, David. *Annals of Annapolis, Comprising Sundry Notices of That Old City From the Period of the First Settlements in its Vicinity in the Year 1649, Until The War of 1812*. Baltimore, Maryland: Cushing Brothers, 1841. Reprint 2010.

Riley, Elihu S. *A History of Annapolis, in Maryland, 1649-1887*. Annapolis: Record Printing Office, 1887.

Riley, Elihu Samuel. *Annapolis, "Ye antient (sic) capital of Maryland."* Annapolis, Maryland: Annapolis Publishing Company, 1901.

Risjord, Norman K. *Builders of Annapolis, Enterprise and Politics in a Colonial Capital*. Baltimore: Maryland Historical Society, 1997.

Russo, Jean B. & J. Elliott Russo. *Planting an Empire, The Early Chesapeake in British North America*. Baltimore, Maryland: The Johns Hopkins University Press, 2012.

Stearns, Harold E., Editor. *America Now, An Inquiry into Civilization in the United States, By Thirty-six Americans*. New York, N.Y.: Charles Scribner's Sons, 1938.

Stevens, William Oliver. *Annapolis: Anne Arundel's Town*. New York: Dodd, Mead & Company, 1937.

Thomas, Evan. *John Paul Jones: Sailor, Hero, Father of the American Navy*. New York: Simon & Schuster, 2003.

Thorsness, Leo. *Surviving Hell, A POW's Journey*. New York, N.Y.: Encounter Books, 2008.

Thruston, Mynna. *A Day in Historic and Beautiful Annapolis*. Hagerstown, Maryland: Hagerstown Bookbinding & Print Co., 1916. Third Edition, 1924.

Timberg, Robert. *State of Grace, A Memoir of Twilight Time*. New York, N.Y.: Free Press, 2004.

Toews, Rockford E. *Lincoln in Annapolis, February 1865*. Annapolis, Maryland State Archives, 2009.

Twoling, Dorothy, Editor. *George Washington's Diaries, An Abridgment*. Charlottesville, Virginia: University of Virginia Press, 1999.

Unger, Harlow Giles. *The Unexpected George Washington: His Private Life*. Hoboken, New Jersey. John Wiley & Sons, Inc., 2006.

Warner, William W. *Beautiful Swimmers, Watermen, Crabs and the Chesapeake Bay*. New York, N.Y.: Back Bay Books/Little, Brown & Company, 1976.

Warren, Mame. *Then Again... Annapolis, 1900-1965*. Annapolis, Maryland: Time Exposures Limited, 1990.

Warren, Mame and Marion E. *Maryland Time Exposures, 1840-1940*. Baltimore, Maryland: The Johns Hopkins University Press, 1984.

Warren, Marion E. and Mary G. Warren. *Annapolis Adventure, Present and Past*. Annapolis, Maryland: Whitmore Printing, 1970.

White, Clarence Marbury Sr. and Evangeline Kaiser White. *The Years Between, A Chronicle of Annapolis, Maryland 1800-1900*. New York: Exposition Press, 1957.

Williams, Rosemary F. *Maritime Annapolis, A History of Watermen, Sails & Midshipmen*. Charleston, South Carolina: The History Press, 2009.

MISCELLANEOUS SOURCES

A Brief History of Reynolds Tavern. A paper prepared by the Staffs of Maryland Historical Trust and Historic Annapolis, Inc.

Ageton, Arthur A.: "Annapolis, Mother of Naval Men." U.S. Naval Institute Proceedings. Annapolis. October 1935.

Annapolis High School Class of 1952 50th Anniversary Reunion Booklet of Memories.

Building Towards the Fourth Century. Annapolis Historic District Design Manual. By Dale H. Frens, AIA, and J. Christopher Lang.

"Happy Birthday Mr. Jefferson: Reflections on Remembering Time and Place—Thomas Jefferson in Annapolis, Maryland, November 25, 1783—May 11, 1784." Blog by Edward Popenfuss, Former Maryland Archivist.

"The Maryland Constitutional Convention of 1776." Archives of Maryland, Documents for the Classroom.

One Hundred Years of Vanity Fair. Vanity Fair, October, 2013.

"Pip & Zastrow: An American Friendship." A film by Victoria Bruce & Karin Hayes. Urcunina Films, 2008.

The Evening Capital, Annapolis, Maryland:
> December 1, 1942
> December 7, 1942
> December 31, 1942
> January 30, 1943
> August, 15, 1945
> February 23, 1953

"Extra! The Pages of the *Evening Capital* from the Depression to the End of World War II." 1991.

The Road to Rome. U.S. Fifth Army Publication, 1944.

"1952 Wake," Annapolis High School yearbook.

INDEX

OTHER
ANAPHORA LITERARY
PRESS TITLES

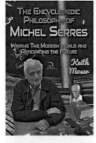

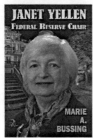

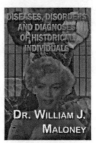

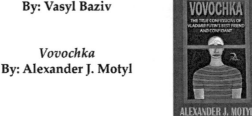

PLJ: Interviews with Gene Ambaum and Corban Addison:
VII:3, Fall 2015
Editor: Anna Faktorovich

Architecture of Being
By: Bruce Colbert

The Encyclopedic Philosophy of Michel Serres
By: Keith Moser

Forever Gentleman
By: Roland Colton

Janet Yellen
By: Marie Bussing-Burks

Diseases, Disorders, and Diagnoses of Historical Individuals
By: William J. Maloney

Armageddon at Maidan
By: Vasyl Baziv

Vovochka
By: Alexander J. Motyl

CPSIA information can be obtained
at www.ICGtesting.com
Printed in the USA
LVOW10*0441180717
541720LV00018B/765/P

KI

C.1